SURVIVING THE WORST

Patricia Oddo

SURVIVING THE WORST
How to Recover When Your Husband Kills Your Children

Max Milo

Max Milo, Paris, 2023
www.maxmilo.com
ISBN : 978-2-315-01137-7

ACKNOWLEDGEMENTS

To my family

Thanks to you,
Rico and Pascale,
Thierry and Claire,
Sylvie and Fred,
Dad and Mom,
Caroline, Vincente, Aubrée, Marielle and Pascaline, my nieces,
Bastien, Simon, Julien, Romain, Valentin and Victor, my nephews,
and, of course, Thibault and Angelique, my darling children.

I needed you and you were there. Together, we stood up to the trauma, each in our own way... and we did. In fact, we protected each other.

Thanks also to Thierry Hernando, who helped me to face the adventure of writing.

In this book, I tell what I experienced, with my own eyes and my own sensitivity. I hope that what I say will not shock those close to me. In no way did I want to judge or hurt anyone. I hope that my friends and family will be free to read this story, and that readers who I do not know will be welcome to read it.

Foreword

Society is governed by codes and procedures, but no method, no teaching, no book, perhaps, explains how to behave in the face of the horror I experienced. In the dictionary, there is not a word good enough to evoke the nothingness in which my family and I found ourselves.

In order to fill this gap, I decided to write my story to seek an answer to the following question: how can one survive the death of one's children? My testimony will, I hope, help to understand the pain of the victims and maybe, one day, to overcome it...

PROLOGUE

Help was there.

Helplessly, I watched with terrible apprehension as the firemen went up and down the stairs of the house. Seeing my distress, they quickly took charge of me. Meanwhile, the doctor was taking care of the children. Then he got into the truck and approached me, giving me the answer I already knew...

*

On September 5, 1990, it was still the summer vacations. Lucie and Sylvain had been at their father's for about ten days and I had to go and meet them at 6 pm.

That evening I knocked and rang the doorbell. No one seemed to be in the house even though the shutters were open. I started to worry. I thought they had gone out to do some shopping. I decided to go to meet them in Saint-Valéry-en-Caux. I ran. I wandered. I crossed a road without checking if a car was coming. More than once, I almost got run over.

Everywhere, my eyes were looking for Lucie and Sylvain. At the corner of every street. Inside each store. At the random crossroads. In vain. I was more and more afraid, I felt more and more bad. Panicked, I went to Dominique's, the nanny: maybe Sylvain and Lucie had stayed at her place?

- Have you heard from the kids? I asked, head on. We were supposed to meet at Jacky's... They're not there!

- No, I haven't seen them today.

- When did you last see them?

- Yesterday, in the communal garden. They were taking a walk. Your husband seemed to be doing well. We exchanged a few words.

I was a little reassured, but more "a little" than "reassured".

I left Dominique in a hurry and went to the home of another friend, Muriel, whose ex-husband had Jacky over from time to time. Her daughter and Lucie were in the same class. Same failure.

As the night progressed, the anguish intensified, it took shape and became palpable. The fear in me went up a notch, like every time I entrusted Lucie and Sylvain to Jacky and he called me at night to tell me, in a terrifying voice, that I would not see my children again. What if the worst had happened? How could I accept such a hypothesis? I could never live without them! My children were my only reason to live. I couldn't imagine a life without feeling them, hugging them, kissing them, hearing them laugh and bicker.

Where were they? What had happened to them? Even though I would never see them again, I wanted to know they were alive. "God, listen to me, please let them be alive," I prayed in the secret of my heart.

That night of September 5-6, 1990, the longest and most agonizing of my life, passed slowly, gravely, out of time. My friend Dominique stayed with me while I was pacing. I called the hospitals in the area and anyone who might have seen or heard my children. I waited, hoped, prayed. All in vain.

On the morning of September 6, with no news, I called the control room of the EDF power plant in Paluel. Jacky and I were both working there, in different departments. Jacky was scheduled to be on shift that morning, but he hadn't hired and hadn't notified me of his absence. In a panic, I decided to call the personnel department at the plant, and I explained:

- I am separated from my husband, Jacky Leroy, and I was supposed to pick up our children last night... He lives in the Ormoie residence in Saint-Valéry-en-Caux... He should have worked this morning, but he is not there!

- Maybe he is delayed somewhere for personal reasons and didn't take the time to warn me? suggested my interlocutor.

- No, I don't think so! On the other hand, lately he has been threatening me by saying that I will not see the children again. I am really worried... I don't know what to do...

- Let's meet at his place in half an hour, shall we? I'll be there.

At about 10:00 a.m., some officials from the plant came to me, accompanied by a locksmith. They opened the door, and I rushed to the garage: Jacky's Renault 25 was there. I felt myself fainting.

At that moment, without wanting to believe it, I sensed that everything I had dreaded and dwelt on that night, everything I had imagined in my most sinister thoughts, everything, that is to say the worst, had become reality. An EDF official climbed up the stairs and immediately came down again. I did not move. I did not try to go upstairs. I did not ask to see the children. I protected myself from this tragic event that I refused to admit, leaving it outside of me, so that it wouldn't reach me.

Not yet.

Not yet.

My employers called the fire department and the doctor, and got me out of the house. I was stunned, terrified, unable to shed a tear or verbalize what I was feeling. I was in terrible pain. I felt lost and I was screaming:

- How are they doing?

I was still hoping that a miracle would happen, that someone would tell me that I was wrong, that everything was fine, that my children were safe... The only answer was that someone wrapped their arms around me and hugged me tightly.

Hector, my friend Maggy's husband, walked by the house and I looked him in the eye. I talked to him and he also hugged me tightly. What did I say to him? I don't remember. I still remember that hug. I knew that everything would change and that my life would never be the same again.

That's when the fire department arrived. Very quickly, too soon, the doctor joined me in the truck. He came up to me and took my hands:

- Madam, there is nothing more to do: your children are dead.

I was torn but not really surprised. I stared at the doctor with the hope that, despite the evidence, the miracle would happen. Maybe he was wrong? Perhaps I had misunderstood his words?

No.

I felt his compassionate look, and he said:

- Madam, I'm going to give you a sedative. This will help you to relax a little, and then the firemen will accompany you to the hospital in Dieppe.

I felt the sting, and the voices trailed off as I lost consciousness.

Part 1: Before

1. The magic of childhood

How could I, Patricia, the granddaughter of courageous and hard-working Italian pieds-noirs, well brought up and destined like them to a peaceful life, have known such a painful fate?

My grandparents arrived in Tunisia at the end of the 19th century, in this French protectorate where there was land and work - in short, hope for a better life. The Italians all lived in the same neighborhood. My father and mother were born in Tunisia. They met through their respective families and were married in Tunis. My maternal grandmother passed away on the day of Mom and Dad's wedding, and the ceremony was postponed until the following week. It was a terrible shock for my mother, especially since her wedding was held in the same church where her mother's funeral ceremony had taken place. My mother spoke sadly of what should have been the happiest day of her life. This tragedy turned her life upside down.

When she was talking about life in Tunis, mom used to say:

- In Tunisia, life was hard. We were not rich. There was no social security. My mother was very sick, so I had to go to work to buy medicine and help the family. I wanted to be a midwife, but I had to stop my studies to go and do some cleaning.

Her voice trembled when she broached the subject. She often cried.

My parents arrived in France at the end of 1958, following the independence of Tunisia. They settled in La Rochelle, where one of my father's brothers lived. They lived in Angoulins-sur-Mer. My father liked to recall his past as an amateur footballer, pointing out that the club that had recruited him provided accommodation for them. Today, I know how much courage and perseverance it took for them to leave everything and go far away from the place where they were born.

Mom was - she died in 2006 - a discreet, reserved person, who only gave her trust to those who deserved it. She was a beautiful woman, with nice shapes. None of us inherited the color of her blue eyes that lit up her face. Mom was not very talkative. Her voice was soft but firm when needed.

Dad, 84 years old as I write this, is a fairly tall, slim man with a dark face and dark eyes. He is courageous, reliable and faithful. He is a person who likes to show off. He likes to appear. This is not a judgment: he is like that, with his great qualities and his small defects. My parents formed a couple that at first sight was a bit mismatched, but in reality they complemented each other very well.

As for me, I was born in 1959 in La Rochelle and my brother Eric, known as Rico, in the same city a year later. I made my first steps the day of his birth. I even bit him, the first time I approached him. We still laugh about these stories.

At the beginning of 1962, we left for Chartres where four of my father's sisters lived. There was work there, they told us: hence another move - one more - and a new uprooting for my parents.

My second brother, Thierry, was born in December 1962. He was a quiet child but often sick. He needed a lot of attention and care. The fourth and last of the siblings, Sylvie, was born in 1965. I was six years old. When Mom came back from the maternity ward, I remember being introduced to my little sister. When I entered the room, I was surprised to see this baby waving and crying so hard. I was probably expecting to see a baby like the one I had as a toy. Frightened, I called out to my mother:

- If that's it, little sister, I'm out of here!

*

After the little incident in the maternity ward, I quickly changed my mind. I felt I had a great mission when my sister was entrusted to me. I still remember when I was giving her a bottle, with my legs stretched out and Sylvie cradled in my arm.

I remember another story. Rico and I went to the same school and we went together. One morning, the collar of his blouse was crooked and I said to him:

- How badly you are dressed!

I went up to him and put his collar back on. I was like a little mom to him!

Rico was a reckless child who was not afraid of anything. Even as a child he defied the rules, and was often punished for it. This was the case at school, but also at home.

1. The magic of childhood

At the time, we lived in an apartment in Beaulieu, a working-class district of Chartres where my parents had managed to integrate. In the household, my father was the only one working and, to go to the factory, which was a few kilometers away, he rode a moped. It was only in 1966 that my parents bought their first car. What an event! That same year, they bought a washing machine. This purchase transformed my mother's life, making it more comfortable: until then, she washed and wrung out her sheets by hand.

That same year, we went on vacation for the first time. We went to Argelès-sur-Mer with neighbors from the building who had become friends. The photos of the time show a beautiful adventure: we were *camping*, enjoying the sea every day. We were free to roam around outside all day, we had beautiful colors.

The following years, we went to Spain, Italy and the island of Ré. It was the time of wild *camping*, campfires and waking up with our feet in the water. What a great time in my life!

*

I was ten years old when my mother decided to find a job. She started working as a cleaner in a factory in Chartres and soon she was hired in the production part. In the 1970s, the legal work week was much longer than today. In addition, our parents accepted overtime on Saturdays. However, my father did not appreciate my mother working, and dinners were tense when she talked about her day.

I soon found myself alone with my brothers and sister for a few hours, sometimes even the whole Thursday. We went to two schools very close to each other. I would drop my sister off at the kindergarten before going to class. Too soon, I was given the role of second mother, a role that I took to heart, without having the choice and without understanding the risks, probably because I needed to feel important and loved.

At the time, I was a quiet, studious, well-behaved child who didn't cause problems. I excelled in school. I excelled in reading, history and geography. I was less passionate about science and math. If we were talking about a faraway country during class, I would pick up my globe and try to locate it at night. I dreamed of exotic travel and adventure. The unknown thrilled me. Reading filled my life and fed my dreams. Yes, I read, I devoured entire books during the *weekend.* As soon as the Carrefour store in Chartres opened, my parents went there to do their shopping. I remember that they often bought me a book. It was a real pleasure. Even today, someone who wants to please me just has to buy me a book to prove that they are interested in me. Books tell me stories and tell me about life. They are for me the well of science. I like to look at them, touch them, feel them.

My father, who was going to work abroad, would bring back little souvenirs for everyone. I was always entitled to my local doll in traditional costume and I had a nice collection of them at the time. How happy I was to look at these characters from different backgrounds than mine!

On the heart side, I had my first love at the age of 7. His name was Alain and he was about twenty years old. My parents were next door neighbors with his. He was in the military, and when he came back on leave, he always gave me a lot of time. I thought he was handsome in his outfit! Unfortunately for me, he was dating a beautiful young woman of Spanish origin. The wedding was coming up. We were invited to the ceremony and the party. When I heard the terrible news, I felt betrayed and abandoned.

I refused to attend the wedding. When asked why, I remained silent. I remember my mother had to make the decision to have one of my cousins babysit the four of us that day!

Until I was ten, I believed in Santa Claus. I was naive; and that was supposed to suit me. Mom and Dad, like so many parents, would tell us:

- Be good, or Santa won't come.

And then one day Rico told me:

- Santa Claus does not exist. It is the parents who buy the gifts.

- You're really talking nonsense! I replied.

- Well, no. You want me to prove it to you?

- How do you do it?

- Want to know where the Christmas toys are hidden?

Without waiting for my answer, Rico led me to the parent's room and there I understood that he was right: Santa Claus did not exist. I was sad and disappointed. The magic of childhood was gone.

2. The evenings of solitude

Regularly, we visited our time-worn paternal grandparents. They lived modestly. I remember that they raised chickens. My grandfather spoke very little French: he spoke Italian. He taught us a few words and how to count in his native language. He sang operas and we had better listen to him. Otherwise, beware!

Slowly, my parents' financial situation improved, so my mother encouraged my father to start building a house. She was more enterprising and courageous than he was. Also, now that she was working, she thought they could do this real estate project.

The idea became clearer when Mom and Dad decided to buy a piece of land in Morancez. Two families in the neighborhood embarked on the same adventure, and we found ourselves neighbors.

We moved in 1972. We were now living in the country, surrounded by fields as far as the eye could see. It was the beginning of another life. I went to school in Chartres like all the teenagers in the village. Most of my classmates came from farming families.

The days were long, but I loved going to school. We left in the morning with the bus and returned in the evening. The time of the journey allowed me to get to know the young people of the village better. My mother used to ask me to do household chores, which I did without reluctance. I don't remember standing up to my parents. I never disobeyed them.

Did my tendency to be submissive lead me to make bad choices later on? Maybe. And why didn't I defy the ban at the time? Was it fear of my father's authority? Yes, I think I was afraid of my father. More broadly, was I afraid of male violence? I guess so. Because of my father, did I imagine that men were necessarily authoritarian? In any case, I know that I was afraid of disappointing Dad, this adorable man in society, who in private became angry, scathing and intransigent.

This fear has not left me.

No matter what we did, it was never right or praiseworthy. My father didn't accept our choices. He didn't know how to listen, confide in us or express his emotions. He often yelled to express himself, and I know that because of this, today I don't like arguments. I just wanted him to say "I love you" or "I'm proud of you", which he never did. On the other hand, materially, I could count on him, no matter what.

*

We were happy to move into this new house, in Morancez, despite the rudimentary furnishings and the very *kitsch* wallpapers. On the walls of my room was a tapestry with big orange flowers. The one in the dining room was covered with green and gold medallions. The walls of our parents' room had more pastel tones. In the corner of the living room, there was a stone fireplace that, when lit, heated the whole room well. We often met in this room to watch television together.

Mom cooked a lot, and we especially liked her pasta with tomato sauce. Some days, the smell of spices would fill the house, awakening our taste buds and whetting our appetite.

I shared my room with Sylvie, while my brothers slept in the next room. Some time after we moved in, the attic was converted into what would become Rico and Thierry's room.

On Sunday mornings, my brothers, sister and I used to bring coffee to bed for Mom and Dad. We would fight to occupy the space closest to our parents in this rare moment of family togetherness. I would throw:

- I don't have room, Dad, can you move over a little?

He was pushing himself slightly to the left:

- Is this better, Patricia?

- Yes, we are all set, it's good!

Those mornings had a special taste: we were finally together! Mom and Dad would drink their coffee, and the day would begin. I keep a sweet memory, a moment of family unity that reassured me. It was an oasis of sweetness in the heart of a cold desert of rigor: at home, it was not often funny.

- You understand, I don't want anyone in the house when we are away!

- But why? We don't do anything stupid!

Our parents didn't like us to bring friends over, which frustrated me terribly. I looked around at my friends and thought they were lucky.

The meals were silent. We were not allowed to talk. I remember that one evening, at the table, we all laughed a lot. Even Mom was laughing with us. We couldn't stop and Dad had to intervene:

- Stop laughing! Calm down and eat!

Except that we really couldn't help ourselves...

- If this continues, you will leave the table and be deprived of dessert!

We didn't finish our meal and went to our respective rooms. Dad kept his promise, as always: we did not eat our dessert.

*

On *weekends,* I spent a good part of my days in my room, studying, reading and embroidering. Then I joined the women's basketball team of Morancez, with whom I often left on Sunday mornings to play a game. I was already a fighter, a young girl who never gave up. It allowed me to meet new people and to get out of my house. Going out to play basketball was still okay, but my parents didn't like me going out with friends.

When a party was scheduled, I would ask Mom:

- Can I go to Isabelle's? She invited me.

- Ask daddy.

I went to see my father, fearing for his answer:

- Dad, I'm invited to my friend Isabelle's house. Can I go?

- Ask your mother!

I felt sad and misunderstood. Despite everything, I insisted on both of them to get their agreement... and, generally, I spent bad evenings, alone in my room.

Discotheques? I didn't even have to consider it. I went there so rarely, that you can count the nights I went out with my girlfriends on the fingers of two hands.

No, I didn't have a fulfilling adolescence: there were too many prohibitions, not to mention the fears that were passed on to me. That of boys, for example. I got my period at the age of 12, even though nobody had ever explained to me what menstruation was. That day, my mother took me aside and said:

- Beware of boys, you can get pregnant now!

Being pregnant: I didn't even know how it could happen, but I can tell you that it traumatized me. So I looked to my friends for answers. When Sylvie was settled, my mom asked me:

- Can you explain to your sister what is happening to her?

Without hesitation, I agreed. I didn't want my sister to learn about this normal event in a woman's life the way I did.

However, I was not angry with my mother. Today, I understand that she did not know how to deal with us, and that this clumsiness was undoubtedly due to a defect in the education that she herself had received. As a child and then as a teenager, I swore to myself that I would raise my future children with rigor but with a lot of listening, exchange and love.

*

For a long time, I dressed like the boys whose games I shared. I had got it into my head that life was more favorable to men than to women. Probably because my mother worked staggered hours: she started at 5 and finished at 13. She had little or no rest, and she worked hard to keep her house in order. She allowed herself little free time, so much so that she forgot herself. Living for herself was not part of the culture of the time. I was imbued with this very negative example of womanhood and it was only much later that I became aware of my femininity.

My father's path seemed very different: he became a foreman in the factory where he was employed. He was happy with his success and with the feeling of being indispensable.

- Even at night," he used to proclaim, "when there's a problem, they call me!

His new position fit him like a glove, with his strong character. My father never missed an opportunity to breathe down the necks of the employees under his command. I can understand his pride: starting from nothing, he knew how to make a place for himself in the company that employed him. That said, he could have accepted the idea that Mom was successful, too. She would have liked a little more attention, to go on a trip, to receive gifts, surprises...

In 1975, I entered the Lycée Jehan de Beauce, in Chartres, to prepare a BEP in accounting. The following year, Rico went to the same school to prepare a BEP in electromechanics; and my life changed for the first time.

3. THE MIRACLE OF THE SUZUKI 1000

- Tell me, Rico, who were you chatting with on the playground?

- A friend who is in class with me. His name is Jacky.

I passed this young man chatting with my brother in the schoolyard. He was not very tall but, with his blond hair and green eyes, Jacky was rather handsome. He was slim and even very athletic: he was a gymnast, and he didn't hesitate to boast about the results he had obtained. Rico having become his friend, I had the occasion to see again outside the high school this boy who attracted me enormously. His appearance, his way of being, his rebelliousness, the freedom he enjoyed and which contrasted with the education we had received... Very quickly, I had in mind to know him better and, as they said at that time, to date him. What a disappointment to find that he was not interested in me at all!

Especially since Jacky had a motorcycle, a 125, while most of us had at best a bike or a moped. It must be said that my brother's friend was the youngest in the family. He had been raised as an only child, with his sister and brothers at least ten years older than him. His parents were old and spoiled him a lot.

I remember how he looked like a biker, with his long hair, his boots and his slightly large jacket. Every once in a while he would ask me to ride with him, and I was the happiest girl. I dreamed of going out with him!

Jacky was very outspoken, and I was surprised by the way he talked to his mother. What a contrast with the education I had received! His rebellious side amazed me, who never dared to defy the forbidden... He represented everything my father didn't like, and I liked that.

Jacky lived in Chartres, on the lower town side, as the center is called. From time to time, when Jacky would ask us to come to his house for a snack, I would meet his parents. Sometimes we would go to a cafeteria to play *pinball* and have a drink. At the time, these moments seemed more than privileged; let's even say they were exceptional for me who was not used to going out!

Jacky was not very studious, like Rico: it happened that my brother asked me, the day before for the next day, to write his French paper. Once the subject was "torture". I was idealistic and had great theories about it. I wrote Rico's essay, and the next day at ten o'clock Jacky copied the paper, changing a few words, but not changing the turn of phrase. The teacher immediately realized the deception and gave both of us a zero score!

Time passed, but Jacky was not interested in me. So I moved on... I met other guys, without much success. It was hard for me to believe in love. I didn't believe in it at all. I was afraid. I didn't know what it was yet, but I was afraid. I probably didn't trust myself, life, the other person.

In 1978, I left high school and found a job as an accountant. I worked in three different sites with the PEP 28, an association that managed summer camps and a CMPP (Centre médico-psy-chopédagogique). I liked working there because my colleagues were pleasant and the atmosphere was friendly.

I was still living at home with my parents and in order to emancipate myself, I took my driving test. It was my priority because, for me, driving was synonymous with freedom and travel. Very early, I wanted to become independent without daring to take the step. I knew that my father did not want me to leave home: in his mind, a girl was leaving the family cocoon to get married. As this project was not on the agenda, I stayed at home with my parents...

*

One Saturday in September 1979, I saw a big Suzuki 1000 motorcycle parked in front of the house.

Just after, someone knocked on our door. Who was it? Curious, I went to open the door... and Jacky reappeared in my life in an unexpected way, the year I turned 20. He had just finished his military service, which he had done in the Paris fire department. At that moment, my heart raced and I remembered all the times we had spent together with Rico. I remembered how attracted I was to him then... and I stood there, disillusioned, with the idea that he wasn't interested in me.

- Hello, I'm here to see Rico...

Jacky came into the kitchen, greeted my parents and, at their invitation, sat down with us at the table. Dad and Mom asked him, without indiscretion:

- What do you do for a living, young man?

- I work for EDF, at the Gennevilliers power plant in the Hauts-de-Seine region.

- Bravo, this is a good situation!

Meanwhile, I went about my business, not caring much about our unexpected visitor. When he left, Rico not being back, I invited Jacky to our respective birthdays, which we were to celebrate the following week. He agreed to come:

- I'd be happy to," he replied in a casual tone.

After his departure, Sylvie was quick to comment on the event:

- Did you see that? He kept looking at you!

- Really? I didn't even notice.

I was flattered by my sister's remark, and I slept very well that night. Then Jacky went out of my mind... only to come back the following Saturday.

*

It was at this birthday party that we met again. Many friends were there, as well as cousins. All these people were gathered in the living room of our house, transformed for the occasion into a party room. I helped my mother to prepare the meal, serve and serve the dishes. We loved to entertain and when we had guests, we used to cook ourselves. I was very busy and spent little time at the table. I hadn't chosen my seat, but I found myself sitting not far from Jacky, who said to me:

- Ah, Patricia, here ! I'm glad to see you.

And there, to the point, he offered me a pretty bouquet of roses, my favorite flowers. I was very happy to see him again... until I realized, a few minutes later, that I had nothing special to

4. The fateful question

After this first *flirtation*, Jacky and I continued to see each other.

Because of his professional activity, Jacky lived part of the week in the Paris region. He would come back to Chartres when he was off. When he was away, I would write him long, passionate letters telling him how much I missed him and what we could do on the *weekend*! My lover never sent me a reply: he was not a great romantic, really not... He did not express his feelings and emotions much. His feminine side, so to speak, was not developed at all.

Convinced that he would learn to show affection, I was nonetheless flattered by his interest in me when we were near each other. I must admit that this was enough for me. I thought, "Maybe this is what loving is all about..." His reserved nature did not prevent me from being madly attached to him. I was as blue in the face as you can get - in fact, I think I*'m* still blue in the face!

Sometimes, in spite of myself, I wondered what it was to love. My parents were a couple who were not very demonstrative. Never a kiss, never a gesture of affection, never a Valentine's Day gift. In this respect, my boyfriend's attitude frustrated me, yes, but it didn't shock me more than that. I clung to the hope that he would change. Especially since there were some magical moments! The woman who never went on a motorcycle stuck against Jacky doesn't know what shivering with pleasure and excitement means... Although, afterwards, I repressed for a long time, without wanting to, our most beautiful moments of complicity, some of them come back to my memory, as vivid as the first day.

For example, I remember the *weekend I* spent at the 24 hours of Le Mans - an extraordinary moment if ever there was one. I never thought I would have such an adventure!

I also remember with emotion our motorcycle trip to the sea in Normandy.

I also remember that on the evening of my 21st birthday, Jacky made a reservation for two at the Estocade. At the time, it was one of the most famous places in Chartes. It was located in the lower town, on the banks of the Eure. After the meal, we walked hand in hand along the river. I have not forgotten.

I remember especially our first vacations, in Sainte-Marie-la-Mer, near Perpignan, during which I finally discovered the South of France. For Jacky, these excursions were nothing exceptional, as his parents had accustomed him to them. For me, who had not had the opportunity to experience such excursions, it was a dazzling experience. In spite of my companion's modesty, I knew that he was happy to open me to such experiences, and his joy reinforced mine.

In Sainte-Marie, I also remember our nightly walks along the harbor, and the wild tennis matches we played in doubles, with a couple we met there, with whom we had become friends (Jacky was an excellent player!). And I remember my surprise when he offered to put sunscreen on my back - an offer he repeated every day. No pun intended, but I was very touched by his attention!

In short, the months passed, between hugs and silences. Beyond our complicity as a couple, would I have liked to hear the phrases I was dreaming of, such as: "You are the woman of my life" or, failing that, more down-to-earth words, such as: "You are great" or, *at the very least*, "You matter to me"? Yes, yes, yes, a thousand times yes! Alas, the words never came. Jacky seemed unable to say them. I thought it best not to ask for them. I am not sure they would have come; and, supposing Jacky had managed to get them out of his mouth, if only to have peace, what would they have tasted like then?

*

In March 1981, just after the wedding of my brother Rico with Nathalie, I was invited to Jacky's house. On the kitchen table there was a plate of small peeled grey shrimps. We went to the table. I was about to serve myself, when my future mother-in-law stopped me:

- No, it's Jacky's plate!

My lovely hostess returned with another plate of shrimp... unpeeled. I was speechless, and Jacky said nothing. I am shocked at both the mother's attitude and the son's non-reaction. For them, everything is normal. I am so stunned that I have never dared to bring up this incident again.

It was on that day that I understood the relationship between Jacky and his mother. The son was the main interest of his dear mother. He knew it and took full advantage of it, without complex or limit. He relied totally on her. She took care of all his affairs, from the housework to the cooking, including his accounts and the administrative hassles. There was, no doubt, a practical side to this; but how could an adult accept the price to be paid for this "freedom", namely to be vampirized by his own mother?

*

Some time later, my future mother-in-law asked:

- Where do you go on vacation?

- In Corsica, I replied spontaneously.

- I am not talking to you, I am talking to my son!

Jacky did not react either. Unable to revolt, I nevertheless grumbled:

- Well, logically, the answer should be the same...

Then while I was clearing the table, the hostess engaged me on an unexpected topic:

- It's high time you got married. I talked to Jacky about it. He agrees.

I looked at her, stunned. Why was she proposing to me and not my boyfriend? As usual, I was ambivalent. On the one hand, marrying Jacky was my dearest wish, the first step towards the logical continuation of what I hoped for: having children, building my house, etc. On the other hand, that the mother would marry me was not a good idea. On the other hand, the fact that the mother proposed to me instead of her son hurt my feelings.

Nevertheless, the two sides were not equal. I was much more excited about the prospect of marriage than I was about the method. On the one hand, because Jacky would officially be my husband (what a joy!). On the other hand, because, thus, I would be able to leave the house. My parents would never have accepted that their daughter live with a man without having gone before the mayor and the priest. The icing on the cake of my joy was that Jacky would be transferred to Normandy. In other words, I was leaving Chartres. I was longing for this with all my heart. I wanted to change region and life. This opportunity offered me both. In Chartres, I was suffocating under family pressure. A marriage project gave me the freedom I had been dreaming of for a long time.

All the more so because, deep in my soul, there was a hope that, away from his family, Jacky would change. He would open up more, he would finally express his feelings, and we could live happily ever after. I, who always tend to hope that the best will come soon, how could I refuse such a chance?

*

The wedding date was set for June 5, 1982. The two families got together to plan the event. Right away, my future mother-in-law spoke up, her voice confident and full of innuendo:

- You know, the family is not very big. There won't be many of us at the meal...

- Don't worry," replied my mother, who took the hint. We will take care of the financing for our family and friends.

Realizing that Jacky's mother had just shamelessly flaunted her avarice, I decided, flabbergasted, to pay for some of the expenses myself and to get involved in the practical organization of the day. It's in my nature: I'm a doer! I booked the village hall in Sours, not far from our house. I bought the decorations that would adorn the place. I ordered the favors that I would give to each of the guests. Finally, I went to a printer to choose the invitations.

I liked one design more than the others: it was of a couple strolling through fields. The colors were in pastel tones that I liked, and I left with a copy.

The following *weekend*, Jacky returned to Chartres and I told him about my purchases:

- Look at this! I went to the printer. I really like this invitation! What do you think of it? We can go back and look at it together if you want?

- Well, if you like it... OK, we'll go next *weekend*. You know, I don't really care.

His answer shook me up, but I made up my mind to think that this kind of detail was exclusively feminine. A real boy can't be sensitive to it... even if, under the circumstances, Jacky could have made a little effort!

The two families called on a caterer, who offered us various menus. Our choice was a fish entrée, meat in sauce with vegetables, salad, cheese... and the inevitable pièce montée, on which were placed two figures representing the bride and groom. I managed to drag Jacky to the jewelry store to pick out our wedding rings - and I didn't expect to have such a beautiful moment in that store. My groom had decided that we would wear the same ring. He chose the one I specifically liked, and he settled on both rings.

In short, thanks to our combined energies, everything was ready for the big day!

*

On June 5th, the weather was nice and warm. It was going to be a beautiful day. Like all the brides, I went to the hairdresser on Saturday morning to have my hair done in a pretty bun. Then the beautician did my makeup. I had a very beautiful lace dress. The nieces of Jacky were bridesmaids. They were all dressed the same. Their role - which they took to heart! - was to hold the veil.

A hundred people had been invited. It should have been one of the most beautiful days of my life, but my heart was not in it. A strange feeling came over me: that I was not in the right place, that I was not in agreement with myself. So much so, that when the mayor asked me at the time of the commitments:

- Do you, Patricia, take Jacky to be your lawful wedded husband?

the time seemed long.

I wanted to say no.

Without knowing why.

An intuition cannot be explained. Only the obvious remains: at that moment, I almost cancelled my wedding. Then, very quickly, in my head, various thoughts crossed my mind: "What will Jacky, the family and everyone think? How can I do it? Everything is organized! All these expenses incurred..."

So I didn't dare say "NO", or even "no". However, I did not say a 100% "yes". Rather, I said a timid, hesitant, difficult "yes", which came out of my mouth almost in spite of myself, but which I repeated almost without hesitation in the church where a priest received our consents. Perhaps this is nothing exceptional. Maybe many young women have the same fear of commitment at the crucial moment! Trying to convince myself of this, I erased this hesitation from my memory, and life went on.

5. The beautiful days

A few days after the ceremony, we organized the move to Normandy. I gave my resignation to follow Jacky. I felt a great sense of loss when I left my colleagues who had become friends. However, my mind was elsewhere: I had already moved on.

Happy with this new beginning, I felt like I was growing wings. We went to the store to pick out furniture for our new home: an oak highboard, a jam cabinet and a bookcase.

- What is the delivery time?

- About six weeks, the vendor replied.

- We'll be *camping* at home for a while, I concluded enthusiastically.

- We are not made of sugar!

Very quickly, we knew a certain comfort. We lived in a house in a housing estate in Saint-Valéry-en-Caux. We had a large garden that allowed us to enjoy the outdoors as soon as there were a few rays of sunshine, which happens in Normandy from time to time. I was happy to live by the sea, even if it wasn't the French Riviera.

I thought we were lucky to have such a beautiful house, as it was spacious and well designed.

When you entered through the main door, a large entrance served the kitchen and the living room. In the dining room, two large bay windows allowed for a nice amount of light. The wallpaper of this pleasant room was light pink. The kitchen was large and functional, and next door was the laundry room, which was very practical. The bedrooms and bathrooms were on the first floor. The tapestries in each of them were in soft tones, with different patterns. In this house that we rented, we should be able to live comfortably!

Jacky often referred to his salary, thanks to which we were doing quite well financially. He wasn't wrong, I wasn't working; but I had left everything to follow him and I thought his comments were very unfair. So I warned him:

- You know, Jacky, I don't think I'm going to stay without work. I need to go to work, to meet people, to feel useful; and then, it will allow us to live better!

My husband offered me his favorite answer: silence.

I had become dependent on him. I never spoke with him about this discomfort. Why not? Fear of confrontation, no doubt: I had never succeeded in asserting myself against my father's authority. I would have struggled just as much with my husband's authority, but I kept my best weapon in the face of his mutism: hope!

*

In spite of our differences in character, I believe that we loved each other. We felt a very strong physical attraction to each other;

and we were as happy as we were greedy to discover the infinite possibilities that our bodies offered us, and that our education as much as our parents had hidden from us for a long time.

At the end of June, we left for our honeymoon in Italy. We went to Venice, a dream destination for all lovers! During the day, we strolled in the alleys, passing from one square to another. We went to the Bridge of Sighs, the Rialto Bridge and the San Marco square. I found this city very lively and original: Venice is so steeped in history, that I loved staying there.

We hadn't yet tried the inevitable gondola ride: I found this romantic idea a bit overrated, but we had just gotten married. So why not?

- Jacky, we could visit Venice by gondola. This is our chance. We could see the city with a different glance.

- Stop with your midget ideas! Don't you have anything more original? And it's too commercial !

- Yes, it's true... But this is our honeymoon," I whispered sheepishly.

Jacky did not want to fulfill my dream. I was sad.

We left Venice for Rome, where we stayed for a few days in a *campsite* near the capital.

We were in 1982, the year of the World Cup and the semi-final between France and Germany. We watched the game under a huge tent set up for the occasion. We were very excited. We had already watched the previous matches at the bar overlooking the beach, on a small television around which all the soccer fans, whatever their nationality, were gathered in a joyful and passionate atmosphere.

Italians, Germans and French were there, mixed and tight to watch the game. The atmosphere was crazy. Glass after glass of beer was being emptied around us. When Harald Schumacher, the goalkeeper of the German team, slashed the Frenchman Patrick Battiston, an explosion of anger shook the audience. Jacky was not the last to insult the referee by shouting:

- Sold out! He's gonna steal the game! Rotten!

Indeed, the French team lost; and yet, in spite of this disappointing outcome, we spent an unforgettable evening. Even though he was revolted by the result, Jacky was happy. He liked to have a lot of people around him; and he loved sports.

Then, under an overwhelming sun, we visited the Vatican, the Sistine chapel, the Colosseum... well, all the tourist places and monuments of Rome. We made friends with some young Italians who were staying in the same *campsite* as us. I had learned their language in my family and at school, and I was happy to chat with them. We spent a few days on the beach and *lounging around;* we had lunch in a straw hut, delighted. Those days went by quietly.

One evening, I saw a little girl jumping around and I approached her. I enjoyed talking to this energetic, fun-loving, talkative child. She told me her name was Angelica. I liked this name very much, but since I was a teenager, I told myself that if I became the mother of a little girl, her name would be Lucie. I loved this name: it was my paternal grandmother's name; it was also my middle name - a sweet, bright and hopeful name!

*

I had some problems with oral contraception. So I decided to stop taking the pill and be careful to avoid the most fertile period. Subconsciously, I think I wanted a child. We hadn't decided, but

I had talked to Jacky, who didn't seem to be opposed to my desire. And yet, one day...

- Jacky, I have good news!

- Really? Which one is it?

- I am pregnant. We are going to have a baby.

- Oh yeah... What a revolution!

The vacation in Italy had pumped me up. We were back in Normandy. This news filled me with happiness. As for Jacky, he seemed happy, but he didn't express it. I would have liked him to jump into my arms, to shower me with kisses, to celebrate with dignity this miracle that is the first child for a young couple! As usual, I expected too much, no doubt. Jacky seemed more pleased to see me delighted and upset than to learn of a news that did not warm his blood.

So I turned to a more sensitive ear. In other words, I called my mother:

- You're going to be a granny again.

- No?

- Yes, it's confirmed, I'm having a baby!

- Great news! Already the second birth of the family!

Mom and Dad were already grandparents to Rico and Nathalie's daughter Caroline.

I bought Laurence Pernoud's *bestseller, J'attends un enfant.* This fascinating and enriching reading accompanied me during this first pregnancy. Thanks to it, I was able to calm my worries and find answers to my questions. Despite this precious guide, I was sick until the third month. My tastes changed: I could no longer drink coffee, strong smells made me nauseous... All these transformations convinced me that my life was going to change.

Then everything went back to normal, and the end of the pregnancy went very well. My belly was getting rounder, the baby was moving and I loved to stay for hours with my hands on my belly. I knew it: soon I would be a mom! Very motivated, I learned to knit and I made layette for my baby.

*

Jacky was not concerned with household and administrative tasks. He preferred to concentrate on tasks more within his reach, such as watching television. He watched it all the more because he was one of the *early adopters of* the VCR - and, at the time, this now obsolete device was no laughing matter! Passionate about new things, he also loved video games.

I managed all the household affairs. I didn't mind because I wasn't working. During the last month of my pregnancy, I was very tired, and when I asked him to help, he agreed to do it. He never put his hands on my belly, it scared him:

- No! It reminds me of Alien!

Lulled by the atmosphere of the horror movies he watched without moderation, he felt like the baby was going to come out of my belly like an alien monster. Too much TV, maybe? But TV was also the occasion of very nice moments.

So Saturday night was a sacred time: we would slump on the couch and watch the Inconnus sketches with relish. We laughed so hard at their parodies of shows like "Télémagouille" and "Perdu de recherche"; we knew (almost) by heart their greatest moments, like "Les pétasses" which we also listened to on video cassette and on record; our laughter bounced off each other, our enthusiasms fed each other... and we were moved, I think, to feel absolutely on the same wavelength thanks to Didier Bourdon's band.

We were both *fans of* Coluche. "C'est l'histoire d'un mec" was obviously one of our favorite sketches of all time, but we were eager to discover his new jokes and repartees. So we didn't miss any of his appearances on the small screen.

Television also brought Jacky and me closer together during the French Open. We followed the fortnight's clay court action with great passion, each of us supporting the player the other was taking down. I was Mats Wilander, Jacky was John McEnroe - I preferred the backcourt game, he was first in line for grumbling at the net; Jacky was Yannick Noah, I was Ivan Lendl; and this conventional bickering also helped cement our relationship.

Yes, television brought us closer; but it was also the place of a terrible anecdote which, even today, freezes my blood. One evening, we were in front of the small window watching a detective movie. It was the story of a woman murdered by her husband whom she had cheated on. Jacky said to me:

- I warn you, if you cheat on me, I won't kill you, I'll put a bullet in your spinal cord. You will be paralyzed for life!

Symbolically, he kept his sinister promise, and I will never stop asking myself if, at all costs, I should not have left him at once.

6. The two loves

Jacky was interested in all new technologies or gadgets and games, video or not. As soon as the Rubik's Cube appeared, he bought one. He spent hours trying to find the solution. He used to get very upset because when he lost, the games could make him lose his temper. But he didn't know how to spend time with me.

I didn't know many people, so I made friends with my neighbor Maggy. We were both pregnant and we bonded over our common situation. This friendship helped me to live my pregnancy better. Maggy was calm, composed, and that reassured me. Her little Florian was born at the end of November 1982. He was so beautiful that I couldn't wait for my baby to be born.

The due date was April 8. On March 22, 1983, at 5 a.m., I woke up in a state of confusion:

- Jacky, my water broke, we have to go to the maternity hospital right away!

I got up and dressed hurriedly.

- The suitcase is ready...

- OK, I'll go get it.

I was delighted: the baby's room was furnished and decorated. I had made many purchases to dress my future child.

We drove to Dieppe in fourth gear. When we arrived at the maternity ward, I was put in a room. The contractions intensified: how I suffered! Lying down was no better. Standing up, I was pacing. I couldn't apply the breathing techniques I had been taught in my prenatal classes. I was having more and more difficulty controlling myself.

Jacky did not seem to be affected by my pain. He was distant with me, both physically and emotionally. I would have liked him to hold my hand, to reassure me. But instead, my husband, the father of the child I was carrying, preferred to humor me. At least, he was trying to:

- It will have to come out!

- Call the nurse, I want to push," I replied, annoyed.

The midwife entered the room and examined me:

- We will accompany you to the workroom.

Many thoughts went through my mind: "My baby is coming soon, what a joy!" But also: "Will I be able to bear all this pain? I am already exhausted..." Finally, all the questions that moms ask themselves, especially when it's the first time!

I was at the end of my rope. So much so, that I could not follow the doctor's instructions. The medical team gave me anesthesia and had to use forceps to release my baby.

*

When I woke up, I was alone in the room. Jacky was no longer there. He had gone home. He didn't come back until the next day.

He had made the choice to work during my stay in the maternity ward and to take days off when I returned, even if it meant not being present during his child's first days.

Still smeared from the anesthesia, I was surprised to find myself in this hospital room. I turned my head and discovered a baby: what was he doing there? Little by little, memories came back to me: I had arrived in the morning, my water had broken... Yes, that baby next to me was mine! A nurse entered the room and asked me:

- Do you want your child against you? Will you breastfeed?

- Oh yes, of course! Is it a boy or a girl?

- A little girl. All is well.

A girl, of course! During the last ultrasound, I had been confirmed; and here she was, in real life.

I spoke softly to him, amazed at this small package that was going to take such a big place in my heart and in my life, without a doubt. I was overcome with a sudden emotion and burst into tears: I was aware of the deep meaning of the word "responsibility". But I began to doubt: will I be able to do it? So I spoke to him:

- Hello, little Lucy. So you are the one I carried, the one I nurtured, the one I waited for with such great impatience. We were only one, and now I meet you. I am happy for this moment.

I put my hand on my belly. How I had loved this pregnancy, despite the difficult moments! And it was already over... I was not about to sink into the depression of the *baby blues*. My fighting and optimistic personality was already stirring: from now on, I had a child to raise; and, who knows? maybe Lucie would help Jacky to change, to assume his sensitivity more, to express his feelings a little more? Nothing could stop the crazy hope that was burning me!

However, from the beginning, I noticed that Jacky was not comfortable with babies in general and with his own in particular. Sometimes, he would overcome this discomfort, change his daughter or give her her bottle, and I appreciated these simple gestures thinking that, for him, this must be a feat not to be repeated any time soon...

At nap time, in the afternoon, I would lie down with Lucie and she would fall asleep against me. I loved these precious, unique moments. I listened to her sleep, her smiles, her babbling. But I was very tired. I slept badly and everything seemed insurmountable: running the baby's bath, shopping, preparing the meal, giving the bottle...

A few months later, my little Lucie had grown up well but was still fearful. She often cried and had difficulty getting used to another world than her own. But her little world was soon to be turned upside down...

*

In September 1983, I discovered that I was pregnant again. After the surprise, I rejoiced in this unexpected pregnancy. I was very, very happy. I love children, that's a fact, and having a second one didn't scare me. Jacky accepted the idea. For him, it was the right thing to do. Maybe it was even part of my role as a housewife: to run the house, to cook for him, to be submissive and to get pregnant from time to time.

Despite this underlying ambiguity, the nine months went wonderfully well. I had my little Lucie to occupy my days: we would go for walks by the sea and I would rest during her naps.

I only wished for one thing: "That this new baby would be greedy, not like her sister!"

Jacky and I didn't communicate much, but life went on smoothly because I made sure that my husband didn't lack anything. He worked; I, as a wise housewife, took care of the house and the garden. Things were set up this way without our having really decided. We were reproducing our respective family models without being aware of it. I didn't ask him for anything, but I still had my big project in mind: to work again. If he thought that having two little babies would prevent me from doing that, he would find out what I was made of!

Sylvain's birth was scheduled for May 20, 1984. The last ultrasound confirmed that it would be a boy. After my little Lucie, a little guy! I was delighted. Jacky was also delighted, in his own way. To celebrate the news over a solid aperitif and a good meal, he invited "our" friends to the house - in fact, *his* friends that I had adopted, namely his work colleagues and their wives, who must have been in the same situation of dependence.

On May 20, I was still at home and decided to call the clinic.

- If the situation does not change, come in two days, I was told.

Mom arrived from Chartres to take care of Lucie during my stay in the maternity ward. This idea reassured me, since my spouse was not very present. Jacky just accompanied me to the clinic on the morning of May 22. The delivery was induced and the birth went "like a charm", *according to* my gynecologist.

I was very emotional when the nurse laid my baby on top of me. I really enjoyed that moment, not having a similar memory for Lucie's birth. Sylvain's arrival was a wonder.

Sylvain was calm. Very quickly, he had full nights. He rarely cried. I had a daughter and a son: happiness... or almost. The essential was missing: the unity of the family. This saddened me. I pushed this feeling of frustration out of my mind. The children were there, and that should be enough to give me energy and motivation.

Lucie was very cuddly with her brother: she took him against her and gave him little kisses. I was very moved by this newfound complicity. My life revolved around my two children. Between baths, meals, shopping and cleaning, I had little time for myself. But it didn't matter: I was so happy with my two loves!

7. The right choice

One day, I had the courage to put on the table an idea that had been bothering me for a long time:

- Jacky, it would be nice to baptize the children.

- You and your good God! Can you tell me what he does, the Bearded One, for the unfortunate?

I shrugged my shoulders, refusing to get into a political discussion that Jacky had a secret for. Baptizing the children was an important, essential, indispensable commitment for me. I knew that my in-laws were not at all interested in religion; for me, it was impossible that my children not be immersed in water, set ablaze by the Light and marked with the Holy Chrism.

I was raised Catholic, but my desire is not simply the reproduction of a family habit. I still have faith today. I think I have always had the certainty that there is a god, although I am not sure what is hidden under that word. There is something great, powerful, overwhelming, that is beyond us and within us at the same time, and I wanted my children to be under the protection of this entity.

- You still agree that they should be baptized? I insisted.

And, just as dryly, I drew my sledgehammer argument:

- I thought we could get the family together at my parents' house. The basement is big. Plus, the attached kitchen will allow us to have everything within reach.

I felt Jacky relax slightly.

- Pfff, do as you like..., he huffed, but you take care of everything, eh!

As usual, anxious not to commit himself, my dear husband left me free to decide and then to manage the stewardship. Hence this gesture of religious tolerance, which would allow him to be surrounded by his family, as he liked, to talk about EDF and motorcycles, and to see again those he loved. When it falls into your mouth without effort, a family feast is worth a religious ceremony! By dint of learning to be a fine diplomat, perhaps I should have applied for the Quai d'Orsay...

*

The sacrament was given to the children in the parish of Morancez. The meal took place at my parents' home, where both families were invited. We decorated the garage as a reception room and installed a stereo to create a musical atmosphere. Jacky was very happy about this! My husband didn't express himself much with words, but he loved to dance whenever the opportunity arose. He loved music with bleeding guitars. He loved Kiss, Van Halen, Deep Purple, the Scorpions and their anthems - "Still lovin' you" or, later, "A wind of change. By listening to them, he taught me to love them, too, even though my heart was not in *hard rock. I* guess I'm a cross between a sponge and a good dough!

Large tables were set up, and bouquets of flowers adorned the buffet set up for the occasion.

That evening, Mom exchanged with Jacky's mother:

- Patricia is looking for a job. She is happy to see herself back at work. She told me that she has sent many letters.

Indeed, I had learned that they would soon be recruiting administrative employees at the Paluel power plant, and I had sent my cover letter to EDF. I was full of hope, especially since it was the right time.

- I don't think Jacky would agree to Patricia working," my mother-in-law replied in a matter of seconds.

As if she knew what her son was thinking, even before I asked her about it!

A few days later, my mother told me what he said. I was surprised, but nothing more. But I thought it best to tell my husband:

- You know that I sent many cover letters, including one to EDF? Are you aware that they are looking for people in the administrative sector? What do you think?

- You do what you want: you work if you want, but I don't change anything in my life. You're on your own with the kids and everything else.

It was Jacky all over again. So I did what Patricia does best: I didn't answer anything. More precisely, I didn't dare answer anything. I had heard the message, and I told myself that I would be able to juggle my professional life and my life as a mother. I thought my husband's answer was very unfair; I was used to it, but I accepted it and took the positive side: Jacky was not opposed to my returning to work.

Especially since I was not unhappy, I had many occupations! I read with pleasure, especially historical epics such as *La Chambre des dames* by Jeanne Bourin, which is set around 1250, during the reign of Louis IX, but also scandalous stories such as *Le Pull-over rouge* by Gilles Perrault, stories of life and beautiful love stories; I knitted clothes for the children; I painted on silk; I liked handicrafts to decorate my house. Nevertheless, I wanted to work for three reasons, only one of which would have been enough: not to become sclerotic in my little world; to continue to dream of building a house, which was unthinkable on a single salary; and to no longer be financially dependent on Jacky, who insisted heavily on his role as head of the family who boiled the pot.

*

My cover letters and *curriculum vitae* aroused interest. I was invited by EDF for selection tests which went very well. Shortly afterwards, I received an invitation for an interview. I was delighted: things were moving in my direction professionally! At least something positive...

The interview could not have gone better, but in the evening, when I came home, not a word from Jacky about it... What a disappointment, once again!

- You know, I was summoned today to EDF!

- ...

- It worked great.

- Oh yeah, so what?

I was angry at his indifference, but I kept it to myself. Jacky wouldn't accept the idea of me working: he REFUSED to let me have a social life. But what was he afraid of? Hiring me could only strengthen our financial situation! When I received the answer from EDF, it was an explosion of joy, at least for me: I was hired at the Paluel power plant, in the purchasing department.

The hiring date was scheduled for early December. Sylvain and Lucie were six and twenty months old. I had to get busy to find them a nanny. I decided that I would choose the person with whom the children would feel most comfortable.

So I visited - without Jacky - three ladies interested in my proposal. The second person I visited seemed to be a good fit: the children were comfortable with her, and so was I. The nanny's name was Dominique and her son, Anthony, was a year older than Lucie. I felt a bit relieved: Dominique seemed perfect to take care of my two little ones, even if I felt guilty about working instead of staying with them. And how was I going to cope with everything that was waiting for me? Thank God I was brave and determined. I had no doubt that I would succeed.

Better yet, despite my partner's lack of enthusiasm, I was happy. My relationship wasn't great, but I was optimistic. Everything was going to change. Of course, the children's lives would change as well. However, I had found a *cool* nanny, and Lucile would soon be starting school... I was looking for reasons to convince myself that I was making the right choice.

The separation from my daughter would be painful: we were so close that we had trouble leaving each other, even for a few hours. With Sylvain, it was different: he was such an amazing, easy-going baby!

The three of us have often taken walks by the sea. I love looking at the horizon and listening to the waves crashing on the shore.

I always knew it was a good place to be, to take stock, to think. Jacky didn't like to walk around. I often wondered if it was the walk or being with us that bothered him, refusing to consider a third, worse possibility - what if it was both?

8. The new life

A new life began. Many people were hired at the same time as me. The management organized an internship to introduce us to EDF, and we had a quick tour of the site. I was working in a large administrative building. One morning, I passed a beautiful young woman, smiling, although she seemed a bit on guard:

- Hello, my name is Patricia. What's your name? Did you just arrive?

- My name is Christine. I recently arrived in Normandy. I come from the Amiens region. I joined my companion, Luc, who lives here.

- Great! Plus, we'll be working together in the same office.

Very quickly, we sympathized and became great friends.

In the morning, I would drop Lucie and Sylvain off at Dominique's house, then go to the plant. In the evening, as soon as I left work, I went to pick up the children. Life was organized like that, and time passed slowly.

Jacky worked three shifts and every other *weekend.* On weekdays when he was at home, he didn't babysit. He rarely went to the nanny's to pick them up and spend time with them. We were not often together. The moments of happiness for the four of us were reserved for the vacations. I remember incredible skiing sessions. He introduced me to this sport I had never practiced, and I admired him as he *skied* down the black slopes. I remember other moments at the beach, where he accepted to play with our two little ones almost like a father hen!

Nevertheless, in everyday life, the three eights did not facilitate life together and the development of each one, Jacky included. I was on my own way. During the week, I went to the plant; on *weekends*, I took care of the housework, the laundry, the cooking, the garden and the shopping, which I did very often with the children, Sylvain in the seat of the cart, and Lucie in the back. While they napped, I knitted for my loves, trying not to think that Jacky would ever give me the slightest compliment for my work.

At night, when they were in bed, we sometimes watched television. It was one of the few things Jacky and I could agree on, even though he preferred horror movies, like The *Shining, which we both* saw, to comedy shows. That oppressive *thriller* traumatized me, and I've always refused to watch movies like that ever since. I rather like stories that tell the lives of women and men where the emotion breathes out, sucks us in and moves us. In this case, it was more the hemoglobin that flowed, and I found it frustrating.

*

The first time Lucie went to school, it went very badly. The next few times too. My daughter would make herself sick. She would vomit so much she would cry and froth with anger. All these changes disturbed her, who was so attached to her daily life and to her mother. Faced with this situation, I felt alone and powerless. I had to meet the school psychologist who listened to me and tried to reassure me:

- Madam, you have chosen to work, it is a very wise decision. Do not feel guilty, your daughter feels it. Assume, move forward and you will see, everything will return to normal.

I could hear what she was saying. Unfortunately, I had no one to talk to, which left me alone with my feelings of guilt. Maybe Jacky and his mother were right: what if I stayed home?

Too bad for my in-laws and good for me, Lucie eventually adapted to the class, even collecting girlfriends. Everything went back to normal. But my daughter remained reserved, sensitive to the environment and, therefore, fragile. She had big brown eyes, pretty long hair and an angel's face. She was a cuddly child with such intelligence that it blew my mind. She was studious, calm in class, attentive to others, a real girl in her world of dolls and pretty dresses.

Sylvain was the love of a child, blond, with beautiful big blue eyes. I marveled at how easily he could adapt to any situation. He smiled and gabbled constantly. He amazed me. He was a little comedian, less concentrated in class than his sister. He collected marbles and small cars. He had many friends.

*

In 1986, I experienced the Chernobyl accident with concern, for the Russians and for myself. The event called into question the organization within the power plant. I had nightmares where I was trying to save Lucie and Sylvain after an accident. I was sleeping very badly and I sensed danger. It must be said that we spent a lot of time at work simulating nuclear-related accidents. Faced with this anxiety-provoking climate, I decided to move towards a more "technical" profile, which would allow me to follow training courses and better understand the risks.

After an interview with the head of the new department, I was transferred to a position that suited me better: I was now working in maintenance, so I was at the heart of the life of a power plant. I was discovering a new world, with many men, especially technicians. I was the only woman in the department and the men looked at me differently from Jacky. This disturbed me but, at first, it didn't go any further. I soon felt very comfortable in my new job. One of my main activities was to enter work requests from technicians into the computer. This made it possible to plan future interventions to remedy a possible anomaly.

On the other hand, the evenings with Jacky did not bring very constructive dialogues:

- Today I went to the engine room. This building is huge. Impressive!

- Really? You went for a walk again!

When he mentioned my professional activity, he devalued it with these words:

- You are unproductive!

He really didn't like me talking about it. So I didn't talk about it in his presence anymore. His conversations, or rather his monologues, revolved around unionism and politics, subjects that did not inspire me, and which he addressed vehemently:

- There are fewer and fewer union members; management will eventually have full control. You should join, it would be better.

- ...

- The bosses are lining their pockets while the workers are struggling to make ends meet. Does this seem normal to you?

- ...

For some time, he had been trying to apply for a more qualified and better paying job: he wanted to become a technician. But he had great difficulty concentrating on learning, and I noticed that he lacked confidence. He failed several times in interviews with his supervisors, which made him feel bad: it was always the fault of others. Very childish reasoning... Despite all this, he managed to become a technician. That day, I was relieved to think: "Phew, we won't have the grimace soup on the menu tonight!"

*

One evening, Jacky suggested that I invite some of his colleagues to dinner. I didn't mind, quite the contrary:

- Good evening, I am Patricia, Jacky's wife. Come in, come in!

- Thank you. I'm Yannick. I am Yannick, and this is Laurence, my wife.

The current went very well between us, and we became friends. The next day, I remembered the evening of the day before with Jacky:

- Laurence and Yannick are very nice! I appreciate them a lot.

- Yes, yes...

That yes was not convincing or enthusiastic. I think my husband envied my professional success and had difficulty accepting my ease in relating to our children and to others in general. I tried to introduce Jacky to my girlfriend Christine and her partner Luc. I invited them to dinner one evening. Unfortunately, Jacky made no effort to make himself pleasant, and the evening seemed very long.

After this failure, I decided to stop inviting people I felt close to. I was so sad... I felt that I was not on the right track with my partner. I felt like I was missing out on my life. I couldn't see myself with Jacky, and the feeling was mutual. Our couple had no future: I liked to live outside, to play sports, to spend time with the children. He liked to stay at home, in front of the TV and his games.

Little by little, I didn't want him anymore, and he didn't seem to have any desire for me either. A disgust of life, of him, of me and of the situation was settling between us: perhaps I had not communicated enough? I had reproduced what my parents had shown me about married life. The fear of the other, of the relationship, of love, of commitment: all that had paralyzed me.

What to do? The children were there, and I didn't have the courage to leave their father. I felt trapped in the situation. "I'll think about it later," I told myself once again, instead of solving the problem.

Life went on. Lucie and Sylvain, work, a little sport, each other's activities, shopping and housework... My children were taking swimming lessons. I often attended their lessons. Jacky never went anywhere. I was proud of them, while he seemed indifferent.

I was still taking on so many responsibilities in the home, but I was feeling more and more alone. My disappointment was *increasing*, while my strength was decreasing: I was getting exhausted, I was slowly dying out. I was not yet thirty years old, and my life seemed to have no future. Fortunately, my role as a mother and my work gave me enough satisfaction to push me forward. To what extent? I began to run away from home, so suffocating was I: as soon as I could, I went out with Lucie and Sylvain.

My sister Sylvie sometimes came to the house on vacation. She quickly noticed that Jacky did not support me and paid no attention to me or the children:

- Patou, do you realize that he spends his days in front of the TV, with his feet on the living room table? He treats you like a slave, his cleaning lady, his cook, the mother of his children, but not like a human being. Not like his wife anyway.

Jacky had a hard time dealing with the noisy games. So much so that he would yell at the children. He had created a climate of fear, and I came to dread family meals: I was afraid of an argument and verbal violence. This fear prevented me from being myself, from asserting myself. I had to protect Lucie and Sylvain from their father's anger. This obsession paralyzed me. Jacky couldn't stand contradiction. He was quick to lose his temper. When he was at home, I made sure that the children remained discreet:

- Shh, don't make noise, Dad is resting!

I was afraid of his reactions. I didn't understand the reasons for this uneasiness, this anguish that invaded me as soon as I thought of talking to him. I was running away from the obvious, from the decision I had to make: would I be able to grow old with this man? I felt that I could not.

That's when I tried to escape in the eyes of some of the men I was with: at least they were interested in me. In short, I cheated on Jacky. There, during these stolen moments, I found a little strength, of life. I dreamed of love... and of having the courage to leave with the children. I wasn't proud of myself, but I didn't know where I stood anymore. I was disgusted. I felt lost, alone, so alone. I was only at peace when I was with Lucie and Sylvain. Without them, I had no bearings.

The situation became so unbearable that, in October 1989, I decided to talk to Jacky about my discomfort.

- Jacky, I'm not well. I don't sleep anymore. The two of us are not doing well. I suggest that we meet again, that we both leave to find out what we want to do... We will leave the children with my parents. You know that it's difficult for me to separate from them, but I'll do it for us...

- Another one of your whims! Nonsense! I have no time to lose! Jacky didn't understand that it was anything but a fad.

9. The need for air

One evening in February 1990, after dinner, I decided to spill the beans. Slowly and calmly, I told Jacky that I wanted to take a *break*, that I was at the end of my rope and that I couldn't go on like this.

- The children are in bed. We need to talk.

Despite my efforts, my voice trembled. I was afraid.

- That's it. I'm uncomfortable. We don't talk to each other... This can't go on. I'd like us to separate, at least for a few months, to take stock...

I kept quiet. I was waiting for some kind of answer: a disagreement, at least his point of view. His reply caught me completely off guard:

- Why not? How long will it take?

- Until August. We will be discussed after the summer.

- OK.

I was flabbergasted. Disconcerted, even. I didn't expect such a reaction. Despite my lack of understanding, one thing was certain: I already knew that I wanted a divorce. I just hadn't found the courage to tell him yet. It would have been too brutal.

Following this discussion, I applied for housing and, in April 1990, I moved into a house with Lucie and Sylvain, 3 kilometers from Jacky's house. My parents helped me to redo the wallpaper and the paintings of my new home. I took the furniture from the children's rooms and some of their things. We were well settled and I was proud to be home. Without these chains hanging around my neck, I felt free, happy, light.

Finally!

*

At first, Lucie and Sylvain were not disturbed. Jacky asked me to have them during his *weekends* off. I accepted. It seemed to me to be a good compromise for my balance and that of the children.

I was serene in my life without him, certain that I had made the right decision. The financial means were no longer the same, but I was convinced that I would make it.

As soon as I could, I came back to Chartres near my family. One day, while my mother was ironing, I wanted to confide in her my doubts and anxieties. Because if, at the beginning of the separation, everything was going well, very quickly the situation had become worse:

- You know Mom, I'm worried, I'm afraid... of Jacky.

- I'm not surprised that you and your husband are not meant to live together. He's so hot-tempered, over the top! Rico and Natalie, on the other hand, are not the same. I don't accept the idea of their divorce! Caroline and Bastien will be miserable...

She spoke vehemently.

- Mom, I tell you about my life, about my fears for Lucie and Sylvain, and you tell me about my brother and my sister-in-law!

- You, it's normal. It had to happen sooner or later.

I realized that I would not get my mother to listen to me, and I kept quiet. She couldn't hear me, so focused was she on herself and the separation of Rico and Natalie.

She spoke again:

- You are all individualists! I could have left your father and I didn't do it for you. I sacrificed myself!

Discouraged, I felt alone with my burdens. Mom's words shook me up: wasn't I a mean and selfish person for wanting to leave my husband, regardless of my children?

*

At first, the children seemed to understand the situation, and our life together was going wonderfully well. As time went on, Lucy and Sylvain's behavior changed. After each new *weekend* spent at their father's house, they returned more and more disoriented. Angry, they didn't listen to anything. Especially Sylvain. One Sunday, my son didn't want to come and eat:

- At Dad's, it's better: we eat when we want and we don't have to come to the table. And then he has a video recorder!

This was not the first time that Sylvain had behaved this way. But, this Sunday, I decided to go all the way, because he was starting to want to run the house like a little despot, and I wasn't ready to accept this posture.

- Sylvain," I told him, "I know that the situation is difficult for you, but one thing is certain: at Mom's, we eat at the table, sitting on a chair and what's on the plate. Dad's is different: you can decide to go and live there, if you think you'll be happier. I'll pack your suitcase and you can tell me what you want. Don't doubt: I love you very much. But I can't let you talk to me like that!

I busied myself with packing a suitcase, and accompanied Sylvain towards the exit. We were on the doorstep:

- You decide. If you go to the car, I understand that you want to leave. If you go back, you decide to stay. Only, if you stay, you come to eat at the table with us.

After a brief hesitation, he came home, and I never had another conflict like that with my son.

*

One evening, when I came back from the *weekend*, Lucie did not want me to kiss her. I asked her why she refused:

- You're mean, Mom, because you don't love Dad anymore; and Dad is unhappy!

Jacky was using the children to get to me... At that very moment, I felt so sad, I thought my heart would stop beating. Now I knew that my little Lucy was sad... It was hard for me to answer him without animosity, but I stuck to my promise: not to criticize Jacky in front of the children.

- My darling, Mommy and Daddy can't live together anymore. There is one thing you should know: the love I have for you and Daddy is eternal. You mustn't doubt it for a moment.

In addition to manipulating the children, Jacky had taken the habit, when the children spent a *weekend* at his house, to call me at night to threaten me:

- You won't see them again.

- Why do you say such a horrible thing?

He would hang up and leave me petrified. Other times, he would flatly refuse to let me talk to the children. I shook off my terror, thinking that I had to live and move on. I couldn't focus on these intimidations. So, as soon as Lucie and Sylvain left for their father's house, I joined my family to escape my anxieties. In reality, I had only one idea in mind: to leave Normandy. I felt trapped by this region and by my husband. I needed to get away.

10. The Resolution

The summer of 1990 and the vacations were approaching. Sylvain, Lucie and I were excited to leave for Quiberon. I didn't know Brittany, and it was an opportunity to discover this region.

The children were enthusiastic and couldn't stand still. We went *camping* with friends for three weeks. My sister Sylvie, my brother-in-law Frédéric, their children Julien and Romain accompanied us. Caroline and Bastien, my nephews, joined us for a week. The meals were lively and joyful. The days passed peacefully, just spiced up by the contagious joy of the little ones even if, from time to time, I wondered with concern about my situation.

I was one of the first to get up, because I liked to enjoy the day to the fullest. Every day I proposed activities to the children: beach, coloring, bowls, walking, cycling along the wild coast through the small fishing villages, Kerné and Kernavest.

Sylvain was whole. He did not cheat. He was always in the game, always testing the adults. Very regularly, my son would ask me:

- Mom, can you sing something for us?

I would hum a Tri Yann or Graeme Allwright ballad. As soon as the song was over, the children would ask for :

- One more, Mom!

Lucie was an unconditional *fan* of Roch Voisine. As soon as the song "Hélène" came on the air, she was glued to the radio.

- Hush, I'm listening to the music," she cried, annoyed. Keep it down!

Like so many little girls, she was in love with her idol. She collected the pictures she found. She didn't sing much, but you could catch her humming shyly.

*

Some friends joined us, accompanied by their eighteen year old son, Guillaume. Lucie was very discreet, reserved and charming. This summer, her heart fell for the young man. In the evening, after the shower, to attract his attention, my daughter put on her prettiest dress. She was moving.

Romain, two years old, had taken a liking to his sister's baby boy, almost as big and tall as him. He carried it everywhere, and Lucie let him have it gently. Julien and Sylvain, the two cousins, bickered from time to time. For example, Julien often took Sylvain's bicycle, which Sylvain did not always agree to lend.

- Mom," he complained, "Julien took my bike and he won't give it back to me!

- Let him have it a little longer, Sylvain: you'll be happy to have him lend you his toys!

All in all, we had a great summer. Yet, in the midst of these carefree moments, Lucie slipped in some alarming words:

- You know, Mom, Dad wants to die: that's why he drives very fast...

Another day, while out walking, Sylvain stepped off the curb and started walking on the side of the road.

- Sylvain," Lucie said, "you are like Dad: you want to die.

Stunned, frightened, it was at that precise moment that I made my decision: I was going to divorce and protect the children. I couldn't stand that Jacky was talking like that in front of Lucie and Sylvain. I could not tolerate it any longer. I didn't want to live with him anymore, it was a certainty

Alas, the vacations were over. My stomach was in knots at the thought of returning to Normandy. Nevertheless, I was firmly resolved to face Jacky. I had no choice. Soon, I had to go back to work. The children were scheduled to go to the nanny. Jacky called me:

- How are you?

- Yes, I'm fine. The vacations went well. The children will be at Dominique's starting tomorrow.

- You could have told me about this before! I don't work for ten days, so why don't you leave it to me?

- How do you want me to guess your *schedule*?

- Well, by asking me.

- And what do I do for Dominique?

- You call it and you cancel it.

I didn't dare tell her how scared I was to call her. I sighed and conceded:

- Okay, I'll drop them off.

I was very surprised. When we lived together, he never offered to stay with them.

10. The resolution

I helped Lucie pack her suitcase. We were in her room when she started to sob.

- What's wrong with you, honey?" I asked her.

- I don't want to go to Dad's!

- My darling, he needs you. Soon it will be different.

I was anxious. I didn't know what to do, between the fear I had in my stomach and Lucie's fear of going back to see her father. As a result, despite our shared fears, Lucie and Sylvain went to his house.

*

Jacky and I had decided to meet to talk about the future, especially our relationship. My husband wanted us to start living together again. On my side, I had decided otherwise: I wanted a divorce. During this last meeting, at the end of August, Jacky understood that I was determined, that nothing would make me change my mind:

- Patricia, I don't care what you did. Stay with me. I am nothing without you.

- No. I want a divorce. I don't want a dog, I want a man!

What had I said? That last sentence escaped me, but it was too late when I realized the impact of my words. Jacky's attitude, who was ready to humiliate himself in front of me, in the manner of Brel in "Ne me quitte pas", disgusted me. I was facing a person I didn't know. Under the veneer, the man I had married was a wimp. Jacky took these words to his face. I could see him lost, I could feel his despair. There was an atmosphere of fear. I was distraught too: I didn't know what to say or do. I looked around and saw my little Lucy in the room. She was looking at us, with her big innocent eyes. I was heartbroken!

Jacky approached and raised his hand to me. Lucy came between us, not wanting to see her parents tear each other apart. Disarmed by his daughter's gesture, Jacky pushed me towards the exit.

- Can I see Sylvain? I implored.

Our son was playing in the next room.

- No, go!

I couldn't even kiss Lucie. That's when I asked him:

- Will I see the children again?

I met his eyes, I was afraid. I regretted the question. Three days later, his answer came to me, scribbled on a piece of paper left in my mailbox:

"The question is not whether you will see the kids again, the question is how to avoid not seeing them again. The ball is in your court."

I read and reread this letter. These extremely violent words worried me and resonated with me. Why had I asked this question? No parent who separates from their child asks that question. There was such unease, such chaos... I was afraid. I couldn't live without them!

*

I immediately contacted a social worker and informed Jacky on the phone:

- I made an appointment with the social services, so that the three of us could talk and find a solution for us.

Without hesitation and against all odds, he accepted my proposal. The meeting was scheduled for Thursday, September 6. As a precaution, I went to see my lawyer, and I mentioned the threats that I felt I was facing.

- Wait until you find your children, then go and file a report," he advised me.

It was Monday, September 3, 1990. Two more days to wait. I had to pick up the children on September 5, at 6 pm.

I never saw them again.

Part Two:
The Eric years

11. The lighthouse in the storm

- Madam, you are at the hospital in Dieppe. Do you know why you are here?

On September 6, 1990, around noon, I woke up in the emergency room. A nurse was at my bedside questioning me about why I had come. I looked at her. I made a lot of effort to gather my memories. Little by little, the memory came back to me:

- My two children are dead... Their father killed them...

I was not crying when I said those words. I was aware of the weight of my words, but I was unable to verbalize my pain and sorrow. I felt nothing. It was terrifying.

The nurse did not answer me.

*

The day before the tragedy, I had called my parents to express my concerns:

- Mom, Lucy and Sylvain are not with me. I am afraid that something bad has happened. I don't know what to do.

My parents spent a long night of anguish and, early in the morning, took the road for Normandy. When they arrived home, they were informed by the gendarmes. My mother literally collapsed. My father burst into tears.

At 12:30 p.m., my sister Sylvie, a nurse's aide at the Chartres hospital, was at work when she received an urgent call. On the phone, a man in tears told her the news. For a while, my sister did not recognize him because he was crying so much. Sylvie and Frédéric, her husband, Thierry and Claire, his wife, immediately took the road to Dieppe. The silence reigned in the two vehicles. The shock was total, the atmosphere suffocating. Rico, my other brother, lived in Tours. He too left hurriedly for Normandy.

My friend Christine visited me in the hospital. During those terrible hours, she was among the first to come to my bedside. A few days earlier, I had spoken with her about my fears concerning my children. After the tragedy, I asked her:

- Did you know that he had a gun?

- No... That's horrible! Where did he get it?

I had heard about the gun in the truck that brought me from Saint-Valéry-en-Caux to Dieppe. The firefighters assumed I was asleep, but I was just dozing. They were discussing the tragedy and talking about how Lucie and Sylvain had died:

- How is such a horror possible?

- With a rifle... You have to be crazy!

These words slid across my skin but stayed outside of me, as my brain refused to be burdened with such violence.

I knew what had happened, but I was out of time, disconnected from my emotions, from my pain. My brain was anesthetized. My heart was beating but I didn't feel anything anymore. It was a nightmare, it was unreal. I was going to wake up, to find the children. It was just a matter of time. These people around me, so sad, so desperate, would disappear from my bad dream. All I had to do was wait, pretend. Everything would go back to the way it was. Lucie and Sylvain were going to snuggle up in my arms again. That's why my words were not in phase with the reality and the magnitude of the drama that had just struck us. I knew that this story was just a bad dream. It couldn't be otherwise!

*

Reality caught up with me in a question from my father:
- Where do you want to bury the children?
A decision had to be made quickly.
- In Morancez, I decided. I want to leave Normandy, I can't stay there anymore.
At that moment, I felt unable to imagine living where everything would lead me back to them, where everything would be unbearable, impossible. I perceived the fragility of my state and, at the same time, the strength that animated me.
- And what about Jacky, what are you doing, Patricia ?
It was the first time my husband's name was mentioned. We had never mentioned Jacky. Not once did I ask about him. Spontaneously, I let go:
- Let's bury it with them.
This decision imposed itself on me with clarity, with lucidity: survival instinct? intuition?
- Are... are you sure?
- Yes, I'm sure. I'll leave them together.

11. The lighthouse in the storm

This answer surprised everyone. The members of my family looked at each other in amazement: their eyes said more than words.

- I don't agree with her choice," Sylvie disagreed. Patou is on antidepressants and anti-anxiety medication. Although she seems determined, I don't know if she is fully lucid or capable of making sensible decisions.

My brothers and sister came out of the room. They showed their incomprehension at the idea of the children being buried with Jacky. It was only later, with great humility, trust and love, that they finally accepted my wishes.

How to explain how guilty I felt? Jacky's insinuations and the words we had exchanged had led me to believe that I had made mistakes, that I had not taken his threats seriously, that I had left Jacky, that I had cheated on him. I thought I was a bad person. To get even, he "paralyzed me for life", as he had told me, a few years earlier. By killing the children, who had nothing to do with our marital conflicts but who were my reason for living, he knew what he was doing: by committing this act, he wanted to punish me definitively.

They had died together and I did not want to commit suicide in the vain hope of joining them. Nevertheless, what a violence to not be in the same place as Lucie and Sylvain!

*

My brothers, my sister and my parents were in Normandy for a few days to spend some time with me. We were overwhelmed with sadness. I asked them:

- Lucie and Sylvain are dead, it's horrible... But how? I hope they didn't suffer... Tell me: were they drugged?

I had forgotten how the tragedy happened. I tried to convince myself that my children had died in their sleep, without suffering.

In the morning, when I woke up, the events of the day before came back to my mind. My sister Sylvie spent a night with me in the hospital. I remember saying to her:

- I want to open a flower store with you. I would love to do this project with you!

Sylvie looked at me intensely, dazed. Was her sister losing her mind? Or was she rambling because of the tranquilizers?

- You heard me right, I would love to work with you and sell flowers. I love flowers!

- Yes, yes... We'll take care of that. Later on...

The reception at the hospital was exceptional. The medical team surrounded my family and listened to my loved ones as much as they supported me with small gestures of comfort reminding me that I was still alive.

Then a gendarme visited me and asked me:

- Do you know if your husband had a gun?

- No, no... He didn't have one.

- When did you last see him?

In a lifeless voice, I told the gendarme about our final encounter. After my statement, my parents and I drove to Chartres.

In the meantime, I had seen a psychiatrist at the hospital in Dieppe. I remember making disturbing, offbeat and violent comments to him, sharing my thoughts and goals, not always coherently:

- I know that I will have other children... I have just learned that Lucie and Sylvain are dead... I suffer enormously: I am disgusted to be still alive! I am ashamed to be here! But I have hope: I will be a mother again. Do you know that, since I know this, I am no longer in anguish and fear? Anxiety is an unbearable state.

And then, in the midst of this tsunami of suffering, I felt this powerful certainty like a wave rising from who knows where: "I chose life."

Yes, I chose life.

This evidence appeared to me like a lighthouse in the middle of the sea which, during the storm, shows the way to those who are lost. I never looked away from this light, for fear of losing the thread of my story. I had a glimmer of hope. I did not yet know the depth of the darkness into which I was about to plunge, but at that precise moment, on the edge of the precipice, a will took hold of me: first, to survive; second, to live, and to live well. But how? I didn't know. One step after the other.

However, despite my decision to live, I no longer had a reason to get up, go to work and do all the little things in life that stimulate you. A great emptiness had settled in me. An absolute void! I was absent, and I had the strange feeling of being a living dead person. I sensed that the road ahead would be painful and difficult.

Nevertheless, I had no doubt. By all means, despite the turmoil, I would keep my head above water.

12. The long journey

My parents and I returned to Chartres on September 8. Together, we prepared the funeral that would take place at the church in Morancez. I chose a large heart for the grave, with two swallows drawn on it. I immortalized the eternal love I felt for my two angels.

Next to it, on another marble heart, I had this text engraved that I had written...

No smile is so tender
than those you addressed to me.
As I hurriedly reached out
arms to cherish you and tell you
the story of the Sandman and Tom Thumb,
one morning, two swallows came to take you away
for a long journey.
Since then, every morning, my first thought
is to chase away the clouds.

I could have left the preparation of the ceremony to others, but I absolutely wanted to participate in the organization. I invested myself as best as I could. It was essential for me to accompany Lucie and Sylvain in their last little house.

I didn't want to attend the closing of the coffins, but I insisted that my children have their favorite stuffed animal with them. Lucie wore the earrings that Sylvie had given her from her aunt's baptism.

*

The funeral took place on September 11, 1990. Nearly twenty-eight years later, I don't remember every moment, but I do remember doing what I had to do as a mother.

The time for the ceremony was approaching. We walked from the house to the church. The hearse arrived. After the coffins of Lucie, Sylvain and Jacky were taken out, the whole family entered the church to accompany them. On September 11, the church was full. Many people who had come to attend the funeral were standing or even outside. What a crowd! Friends of my parents, my brothers, my sister, colleagues from the plant for whom buses had been chartered from Normandy... and members of Jacky's family. The assembly was serious and silent, the atmosphere was heavy.

I was overwhelmed by the pain and at the same time carried away by the great strength communicated to me by each of the participants. I was aware that family, friends and colleagues had come for the children and for me.

I had to pay a worthy tribute to my Lucie and my Sylvain. Nothing was beautiful enough to honor their memory, and

I wanted them to be proud of me. I felt I had a mission: to make this goodbye a success.

Here is one of the texts I read at the ceremony:

"Lucie and Sylvain came into my life. It was an explosion of happiness. They were my reason to live and will always be my reason to exist. I already miss them a lot. For them, I will continue to live so that their memory and their memory will not be extinguished. Who was Lucie? She was sweetness itself, calm, wisdom. She was intelligent and very sensitive. Who was Sylvain? He was described as charming, mischievous, always looking for a hug. He was a little boy full of energy and life. My big regret: not seeing him grow up. I love you so much!"

In this church in Morancez, I confirmed my commitment to live. Facing the three coffins, I spoke:

"Jacky, I forgive you your act, even if it breaks my heart. If today I manage to forgive, it is thanks to all those who help and support me in this ordeal. I hope that this forgiveness brings me peace and that Lucie and Sylvain approve of me. I hope that all the people who love me will also forgive him, because I am aware that, with hatred in my heart, I will never find peace.

Yes, I was forgiving.

Sincerely.

Amazing, isn't it? No one understood. I wasn't wiping the slate clean of Jacky's inhumane act. I wasn't forgetting. I was not excusing anything. I was simply giving myself the opportunity to continue living.

I had decided to bury Lucie and Sylvain with their father and not with their murderer. And I, their mother, was not where I was expected to be, in violence, anger and hatred. But what guilt I felt for not wanting to be in the same place as my children!

I had chosen life. By forgiving what Jacky had done, I hoped to be forgiven.

*

At first, forgiveness was liberating. Then, it insidiously mutated into a prison of silence. I didn't know that, by forgiving so quickly, I was abandoning the children and myself. I know today that it takes time: if anger makes life painful, forgiveness is the way out. In order to survive, I jumped the gun, I forgave too quickly. So I entered, without my knowledge, into a long and deep path of guilt and fury against myself that lasted twenty-five years.

Nevertheless, at the time of the burial, I was bathed in the music of "The Big Blue" which inhabited the church during the blessing of the bodies. We loved that movie so much... The men of the family carried the coffins out. There was such emotion!

I remember following the hearse to the cemetery next to the church. I felt alone, but I knew my family was close by. That made me feel better. The moment of burial of the children's bodies was a heartbreaker. I became aware of the physical separation. For a moment I felt like being sucked into the existential void that was invading me.

At the end of the ceremony, Jacky's mother said to me:

- Forget about it, get on with your life. I will never forgive him.

I looked at her dumbfounded, unable to respond to these words that were beyond comprehension.

"Forget the laughter and smiles of my children? Forget their tenderness, their love? How could I forget?"

I felt she was overwhelmed, hurt. She could not be the mother of this man who knew how to organize the murder of her children and her suicide. By not forgiving him and rejecting him, she thought she could continue to live with a lighter weight on her conscience as a mother.

After the ceremony, a snack was offered to the family and friends who had come from far away. I asked Sylvie :

- Can you pick up your kids?

I needed to see them. To see children. To feel their vitality. I had made the choice to live. So I had to reach out to all those who carried that life. My nephew Julien, 5 years old, Sylvie's son, exclaimed when he arrived at my parents' house:

- It's great, it's a wedding at Grandma and Grandpa's!

Seeing all the cars parked, with all the people in the garden, he was astonished. Hence his confusion between the wedding and the funeral...

*

Shortly after the ceremony, I went to rest with my mother. Since my return from Normandy, in the afternoons, we rested together in my childhood bedroom. I was against her, we spoke little, slept much. She supported me. My parents, my brothers and my sister were essential to my recovery. In such an ordeal, feeling loved is essential, and that was the case.

After the funeral, I found myself once again in a feeling of absolute emptiness. I had left Normandy in a hurry, without any

97

luggage, and it was now necessary to go shopping. My sister and sister-in-law accompanied me. Sylvie was literally carrying me, at times, because I was so saddled with medication.

I really enjoyed shopping, where I bought clothes. Lucie and Sylvain loved it when I wore colorful outfits. I continued to dress the same way to remain the mother they loved. It didn't matter if it seemed shocking and far from what one expects from a grieving mother, who is imagined in black, like the Italian mourners: I had never worn black!

Sylvie and Nathalie were anxious to return, so strange did my behavior seem to them. I was talking out of turn, sometimes inappropriate and often exuberant. I spoke loudly, I laughed noisily... Later, my two pillars will explain to me the balancing act they engaged in, seemingly to avoid seeing the newspaper headlines posted everywhere, which evoked my own drama.

13. THE RAY OF HOPE

The day after the funeral, I was taken to a psychiatrist. I was accompanied by my parents. The appointment was brief. After hearing my story, the psychiatrist presented the idea that I needed to rest. I guess the whole family was afraid of my behaviors and afraid for me, afraid that I would commit suicide.

Right away, she asked me how she could help me. I answered indirectly:

- My children are dead. Their father killed them.

I was not crying as I said these words. I was detached from my words and my emotions.

- I suggest you go to a convalescent home to rest. What do you think about it?

- I don't know... I don't see what I can do... I'm tired.

- Yes, I understand.

The shrink called a neuropsychiatric clinic in Touraine to ask if it was possible to take me in. As soon as she hung up, she explained to me:

- You have an appointment on September 13 at eleven o'clock.

The clinic was an old building located in the heart of a forest, 20 kilometers from Tours. I remember it as a privileged, calm, restful place. The center welcomed people from different backgrounds but all in great suffering.

My father accompanied us both on that September 13, 1990. My mother wanted to be hospitalized as well, to stay with me and protect me. In shock, she was taken care of by a medical team, while I was welcomed by a psychiatrist. After a brief exchange, I was taken to a room already occupied by two other patients.

The nurse showed me around: the dining room, the animation room, the infirmary where the treatments were distributed. She described to me the rules to be respected, among others the article specifying not to leave the domain. I had to inform her of my movements by registering me on the activity programs (swimming, walking, jogging, manual work). I had to part with my handbag, with all my papers and the few pieces of jewelry I was wearing at the time.

*

Lunch time came quickly. When I entered the room, all the patients were seated and I had to sit down in the only available space.

- Are you new here?" my neighbor asked. My name is Eric. What's yours?

Eric was a handsome young man, barely twenty-three years old, but impressive for his size. His voice was deep and soft. He smiled little, laughed even less. He smoked a lot. He dressed in dark clothes. He wore a bandana around his neck, like Renaud of whom he was a fan. Eric was a regular here. He suffered from a total lack of self-confidence. He had already tried to kill himself. I found him attractive.

- Yes, I just arrived. My name is Patricia.

- Why are you here?

- My two children died last week. My husband killed them and himself.

Since the tragedy, I had not stopped telling what had happened, as if it were a very banal story, a news item that had happened to someone else and that I had read in the newspaper. It was a naive way, no doubt, but a spontaneous way of protecting myself: this story remained outside of me. At least I thought so...

- I need to rest, that's why I'm here... What do you like in music?

- Renaud, I love it.

- I listen to Patrick Bruel. Only thing is: I took the CDs, but I don't have the player! It's a pity. I would have liked to listen to music.

It was the album in which "Casser la voix" was recorded. This song resonated with me, echoing my pain. Where I was hurting, no one could heal me, fix me. The desire to "break" myself, to hurt myself, haunted me: I wanted the moral pain to go away from me, transforming itself into a much more bearable physical pain.

My table neighbor seemed kind and sad at the same time. He seemed mysterious but I was attracted to him: his fragility was perceptible. After the meal, I went to my room where I got to know my companions. I was unpacking my suitcase to put away my clothes and toiletries, when there was a knock at the door. I opened the door.

A tall, dark-haired young man was standing in front of me. It was Eric: he wanted to lend me his CD player. Embarrassed, I accepted his proposal anyway.

13. The ray of hope

I didn't listen to much music during my stay in this clinic. I soon realized that, despite my initial desire, I didn't have the heart to listen to anything, and even less to sing. The music assaulted me, no matter how sweet it was...

*

The day was punctuated by medication, meals, visits to the shrink, naps and various activities. I spent four weeks in this place. Bonds were forged, with some more than others. I met violent, depressive, alcoholic and drug addicted patients...

I signed up for many activities. I was willing and determined: I went swimming, running, walking, playing ping-pong, doing gymnastics... Some afternoons, I went to the activity room where, among other things, I was offered to paint on different materials. I wouldn't have left the clinic if I hadn't reached the goal I had set for myself: to make seven different plaster masks for each of my nieces and nephews! Each one was a success and a source of pride.

*

Visits were regulated. Nevertheless, my father, my brothers and my sister often came to see me. We would leave the estate and go to the nearest village for a drink. I remember one afternoon in particular. As we sat there, a class of children aged 6 to 7 passed us by. I was looking for a hair similar to Lucie's. For months, with each encounter with children, my mother's heart would rise with hope, only to be replaced by intense pain.

From time to time, I was allowed to visit my mother, who was hospitalized in the nearby clinic. Her pain touched me and oppressed me at the same time. I would walk along a wood to get there: the area around Tours is wooded, it is an ideal place to rest.

During one of my visits, sitting on a bench, we talked. Well, it was mostly her talking! She was talking about Caroline and Bastien, children of my brother and Nathalie who had also separated. She made no mention of Lucie and Sylvain, as if she didn't remember the drama. Perhaps she thought that talking about them would make me suffer? How wrong she was...

On the contrary, I dreamed that she would tell me her memories. I wanted to scream: "Talk to me, tell me Lucie, tell me Sylvain! I need you to tell me. I want that, with our words, our dead still live a little, at least in our hearts!" But I didn't say anything and, of them, she didn't speak.

I was dying to talk about them. This isolation in which I found myself, this heavy silence, plunged me into chaos: did my children exist? Was I going crazy?

My heart, my soul, was cramped in my body, because of the excess pressure maintained by the absence of liberating words. I had to fight not to cross the red line of madness. I knew that talking about them could not bring them back, but only make them live for a moment; and this hypothetical moment was a ray of hope in the emptiness that enveloped me.

14. The synonym of balance

At the end of September 1990, I was still in the hospital. Thank God the weather was nice, and the park next to the property allowed us to enjoy the outdoors. It was easy to go out, as long as we didn't leave the property. I often walked around the grounds. Strong relationships bound the patients together. The distress of each other touched us and brought us closer together.

I remember that, at that time, I paid a lot of attention to my appearance. I dressed in colorful outfits, I hung long matching earrings on my ears. The days passed. We got to know each other among the residents. Some were revealing themselves, others less so. A young girl of eighteen was among the patients.

- My name is Patricia, and you?

- Hélène.

- Why are you here?

- My parents have locked me in here. I don't want to see them anymore!

Hélène was watching me. She knew why I was in the clinic. After this exchange, we spent some time together, during which I told her about Lucie and Sylvain.

- How do you keep going?" she asked me. I don't understand...

- You know, at the funeral, I promised that I would continue to live. I am convinced that as long as I am alive, my children are still present.

I spent more and more time with Eric, with whom I spoke at length. He listened to me a lot. I confided certain memories to him, describing Lucie and Sylvain. I would tell him how much I missed them.

My new friend accompanied me to many of the activities I participated in. It was a real sacrifice for him, because it was not at all in his nature to reach out to others and cling to life. He was more of a shunner of social places, but wherever I went, he was there. Our friendship helped him feel better, at least temporarily. I told him about my plans. My main goal was to leave the clinic.

At the end of September, a few days before his departure, Eric gave me a present: a small white and fuchsia plush.

- I present you Peaudouce, this is how your skin should be.

I promised him to visit him as soon as my health would allow me. He refused to believe me:

- Everyone says that...

- I am not "everyone". Eric, I know that I will learn about life without my children outside this clinic.

- I'm sure you will.

- I want to go home. Reduce medication. Get back to work. Quickly. I need to work again. Then I'll apply for an apartment to be home. I can't stay with my parents forever. And, I promise, I'll come and see you. Do you believe me?

   - I will try.

*

Every day I received a phone call, mail or gifts from someone close to me. I was well taken care of! I was privileged: so many attentions arrived to me, whereas some residents felt abandoned by all! These candies, chocolates, letters, warmed my heart. Each visit was a balm to my heart.

To me who had lost all my bearings, a letter from my friend Christine did a lot of good.

Here is a little note that has no other ambition than to comfort you. It affirms, confirms and assures you of what you already know, a great, lasting and deep friendship. Yes, your grief is immense. No, no one can put themselves in your place. I think about you every day. I don't want to be a counsellor, but remake, build, build a new life, undertake, grit your teeth, live, succeed. You are lucky to be able to relate easily, take advantage of it. You are so alive, surrounded, loved. So many people love you. In some ways, you are like children: you are so natural, so expansive! During these five years, I have always appreciated your sincerity, your frankness, your unselfish friendship, your very positive side and your way of looking at life.

*

I was born on October 1st. The *weekend* before my birthday, I was allowed to return to Chartres. When I arrived at my parents' house, I went upstairs from the garage. With a quick glance, I went around the main rooms, observing every detail. There were no more pictures hanging on the walls of the house.

"Where are my children?", I asked myself. I knew Mom had hung portraits of each of her grandchildren on the walls. And now, nothing. No one left. I shook with panic and groaned:

- Mom, the pictures, where are they?

- I took them out.

- I need to see my children. I can't remember their faces. Do you understand that?

She was distraught. I insisted:

- I beg you to put them back!

At that moment, I felt the irresistible need to caress their image with my eyes, to touch the paper with tenderness.

Mom granted my request and then my parents surprised me by inviting a few friends and family to celebrate my 31st birthday. It was a bold move: I could have refused this gift, but I accepted it. Life was taking over, in accordance with my naturally optimistic temperament. I had chosen life, this life that continued. What a beautiful proof of love on both sides! I was given a locket and I cut out a picture of Lucie and Sylvain, which I glued inside. For many months, this jewel did not leave me. I thought at the time that wearing it, like an amulet, was proof that they were still there. Very quickly, I understood that I was wrong: I did not need a "magic" object to keep my children in my heart. I was feeding on the memory of their kisses, their smiles, their love. I needed this emotional nourishment to continue living.

In order to leave the clinic, I had to show my determination. On October 6, 1990, I was finally able to leave. I had been there for 4 weeks. I knew I would never set foot in the clinic again.

*

Back in Chartres, I did everything I could to regain my independence by looking for a new job.

I also had to write to Roch Voisine, of whom Lucie was a big *fan.* I sent him a letter. For me, it was a priority... I told him about the tragedy, about Lucie and Sylvain, as if he knew them, as if he was a friend of the family. I waited a long time for an answer that never came. Very disappointed, I wondered if this letter had reached him.

I was living with my parents. I needed to regain my strength. It was necessary that I be surrounded, at first. I was on antidepressants, anxiolytics, and sleeping pills at night. Very quickly, I was weaned off the tranquilizers. I continued to do some physical activities, including *jogging.* One day, I went for a run and I ran into my brother-in-law Frédéric, who was employed at the commune of Morancez. I stopped and talked to him for a few minutes. I explained to him:

- I need to get out of the house. It's good for me to play sports, it clears my head. Mom and Dad are always afraid for me. I can't take it anymore. I feel like I'm in prison. I want to go back to work soon and then move back home.

- You'll get there..., he answered without much conviction.

I believed in myself. I knew I would succeed. Besides, I had promised to visit Eric! I remembered the times we spent together.

14. The synonym of balance

A little light had started to shine. I had to prove to my parents that I was taking my life back. Working was a start.

*

Back home, I saw Mom and Dad, distraught, worried that I was late, about to go looking for me. After explaining the situation to them, I asked them to stop worrying, and I dotted the I's.

- I have never thought of killing myself: if I had wanted to end it, I would have done it long ago!

I contacted my department head at the Paluel power plant to tell him about my plans. I was off work. He came to visit me at my parents' house. We welcomed him in the dining room over a cup of coffee:

- Sir, I don't want to live in Normandy anymore. I want to come back and live in Chartres where there is a regional thermal production group of EDF.

- Take time to recover, there is no rush!

- Oh, yes I do! I don't want to be without work any longer...

- Well... If you wish, you can follow an in-house training. In Paris, there are many possibilities.

I imagined myself leaving my parents, my family, to find myself in an unknown universe. The anguish knotted my throat. It was unthinkable to be away from my loved ones!

- No, I want to stay in Chartres. I want to give myself a chance to have other children and to take care of them. With a busy job, I would miss out.

- I see... So, take care of yourself and we'll keep you posted on the progress of your case.

My transfer was accepted without difficulty. Very quickly, I received confirmation of my new job in Chartres.

Fortunately, because my parents were oppressing me. When they saw that I was going back to work, which for them meant balance, they would accept the idea that I could get by.

I was finally going to live again.

15. THE VOID

Before doing anything, I had to meet with my doctor to assess my health and possibly extend my treatment. I chose our family doctor, the one who had known me since childhood. He got right to the point:

- How are you doing with your medication?

I handed him the latest prescription with the prescribed treatment, and commented:

- I am still taking an antidepressant and the sleeping pill. However, I have stopped the anti-anxiety medication and I am experiencing severe stomach and head pain. I think it's psychosomatic.

- Okay, I'm going to prescribe a new treatment for you, and it would be helpful if you went to a psychiatrist. I can suggest some that might work for you.

- Yes, I think it would make me feel better... Sometimes I feel oppressed and so unhappy. I don't understand what could have happened. I should also tell you that I'm going back to work. I think I will get my transfer soon.

The doctor was reluctant. I insisted:

- I really need to work.

- When you have a date, I will offer you a part-time job.

- No, I want to go back to full time, and as soon as possible!

I put forward that it was essential that I have my mind occupied for at least eight hours. The doctor seemed to understand this. But I was afraid to be around new colleagues, afraid of how others would look at me, afraid of being judged. I imagined what some people might think: "If she hadn't left her husband, her children would still be alive."

We reached an agreement that I would return to work on December 3, 1990. By then, I had to meet with a psychiatrist. I was stressed, but I left the doctor with a lighter heart: I would soon be working again!

*

I was frequently visited by my brothers and sister, accompanied by their children, and it was always a pleasure. However, I soon became bored: I couldn't watch a movie or read a book because I had so much trouble concentrating. Like a child, I had to change activities very often, see different people. As soon as my mind was no longer occupied, reality invaded me. Sometimes I panicked. I had a hard time finding any interest in anything. I was a wanderer of the mind. When I fell asleep at night, I told myself that it would be nice not to wake up...

Time passed. Every morning, as soon as I woke up, I became aware of reality. The medication or the treatment brought me out of the denial in which I had unconsciously immersed myself. My memories - painful, necessarily painful - kept coming back, and I had to push them out of my thoughts. Every day that passed was a victory over despair and took me away from the drama. If I had managed to live one more day without my children, I could go on a little longer. But this idea made me feel guilty: how dare I not want to die?

*

In order to organize the move, my parents and I went to visit friends in Normandy. I had to settle some things. I asked my father to go and get all the children's photos. Back from Jacky's house, Dad told me the terrible news:

- Patricia, there are no more albums, no more photos, nothing!

- They were in the dining room cabinet. There are several of them, I was the one who took care of making them.

- There are no more albums. They have been destroyed...

I then realized that my husband had planned everything, even stealing the moments immortalized by these photos. He knew that the garbage collectors were coming on Wednesday morning: he had to take care of destroying the photos before putting them in a trash bag, very early that day.

It was as if Lucie and Sylvain had died a second time. I didn't understand: was I so bad to deserve such a punishment? Why, in addition to taking Lucie and Sylvain's lives, did he want to steal even the images I had left of them? This question still remains unanswered. It was so violent that I was screaming and crying my eyes out. I tried to visualize their faces, but could not.

Later, I picked up some books I had left behind. Among them was an encyclopedia of psychology - I have always been passionate about this art. When I finally dared to open the volumes, I saw that Jacky had circled a paragraph with "PATRICIA" written beside it. It was the story of a man who killed his children. Without hesitation, I threw away these volumes which, however, I was so fond of.

*

As soon as I recovered my senses, I called friends, family, Lucie and Sylvain's teachers and asked them to look for photos of my children. They all reacted quickly, and if, today, I was able to recreate an album of memories, it is thanks to them. There is only one photo left of the three of us together. I am very fond of it, but the most beautiful images remain the memories engraved in my heart, in my memory. No one will ever be able to erase or destroy them.

The only picture of the three of us - May 22, 1990

My father accompanied me several times to the notary's office to settle the estate. These administrative details seemed out of place to me. Nothing was important to me: neither money, nor the law, nor taxes. I quickly understood that it was not by possessing what I wanted that I would regain a taste for life. I had tried the experiment by making a few purchases; but, very quickly, I found myself with the same lack, the same dissatisfaction, the same disarray.

The void.

16. The little fire

In November, I had to bring a document to the notary that was missing from the file. The clerk received me and directed me to an office. We exchanged small talk. I took out the paper while the clerk looked for the file. After placing it on the table, he opened it.

The first document in the folder was a newspaper article about the tragedy. I read every sentence, and every word made me feel cold. It was a very violent reading for me, especially when I read that my children had been killed with a rifle. No one had ever explained to me clearly the circumstances of their death. I had never asked anyone about it. In the office, I walked up and down, not caring about the unfortunate clerk, who was totally baffled... I was angry at everyone, convinced that the truth had been hidden from me. I felt betrayed.

The pain was gripping my chest like a vice. I was in pain and, as always, I couldn't cry. I was in shock. I left the notary's office disoriented.

I joined Sylvie and scolded her, asking her why no one had told me the truth. I had convinced myself that my children had been drugged and died in their sleep, but I had to admit a much more violent reality.

In fact, my brain had neglected the details of the children's death. The separation from Lucy and Sylvain was so intense that my mind had repressed what I was unable to assimilate. The gendarme's questioning could have tipped me off... not so!

I wanted to settle as many formalities as possible before going back to work. The furniture from both houses had been moved to my parents' house. I sold all my belongings, because I wanted to recreate another universe completely opposite to the one in which I lived in Normandy. Nothing would have been possible otherwise. I wanted pink furniture, a flowery sofa, and to live in a bright space.

It was much more painful when it came to sorting out the kids' toys and clothes. I was trying to find their smell. How could I part with such cherished possessions? These personal items brought back so many memories - to Lucie and Sylvain. The thought that they had held them in their hands made me feel a mixture of sweet nostalgia and painful thoughts. It took me several weeks to finalize the sorting. Everything I wanted to keep was in a suitcase: drawings, photos, school books, a few little words scribbled on a piece of paper, a dress, their glasses with their names written on them... It was the most precious suitcase in the world for me!

*

To close the estate, I had to visit Jacky's parents. Sylvie accompanied me. I had taken care of the expenses related to the ceremony, and the family had left me all the goods. Nevertheless,

I was missing some documents. The discussion started slowly, then took a different turn.

Jacky's mother was always very angry. She was a sight to behold, especially since I couldn't help her. As the conversation went on, she blurted out:

- You may not know this, but my son attempted suicide as a teenager. At school, he couldn't stand it when he didn't do well, when people made fun of him. So, once, he tried to hang himself.

I looked at my mother-in-law, stunned. I definitely did not know the man I had lived with...

*

December 3 was approaching, the date of the return to work. I was dreading this moment. I was afraid to meet malicious looks, afraid to work with malicious people, far from my family cocoon. My fears were a real handicap. I was assigned to an accounting department and, luckily, I joined a team of eight wonderful people who made themselves available to me. Most of them were women and became fast friends. After I told the story, I set the record straight:

- I need to talk to you. It's been two days since I arrived among you and there is something wrong.

- Explain what's wrong.

- I looked around the office. I don't see any pictures of children. This is not normal. I know you have children and I suspect that you have made a decision to remove their pictures. Today, I am asking you to take them out again.

- You're right, we had a meeting, and...

- The attention is kind, but I want to know your children. Be yourself and don't change anything for me!

Following this discussion, a beautiful relationship was forged. Going to work was vital. That's why I did my best to be operational as soon as possible. For eight hours, my mind was occupied and I thought less about Lucie and Sylvain. I was working for EDF. I was keeping the accounts for the nuclear power plant in Nogent-sur-Seine. I was no longer at the heart of production. It was a little different from my previous job, but I was working in connection with this world that I knew well.

I found myself near Nicole and Maryse. At noon, I had lunch with the members of my team. I didn't know many people yet, but I confided in Nicole a lot. We were close: I would talk to her about my children, their absence, our walks, their smiles, my joys, my sorrows, my doubts... I was so afraid of the looks of others that I avoided going to the bathroom and I did not make the effort to go to the neighboring offices. Inside me, a feeling of guilt was slowly, viciously taking hold.

To try to reason with myself, I often said to myself: "But no, Patricia, you could not suspect and avoid what Jacky did! He was Lucie and Sylvain's father. A father can't behave like that!" At the same time, a little voice inside me was titillating me and saying, "Patricia, you felt such unease, and you did nothing! If you hadn't left Jacky, they might still be alive. If you had gone to look for them the day before, you could have saved them or at least died with them."

This fight between reason and guilt was slowly consuming me. But I had decided to live; I was sticking to it. From now on, I was committed to seeking peace. Dreaming of this future serenity comforted me.

17. The surprise

I had achieved my first goal: I had a job again! Now I had to achieve a second one: to give myself the means to go and visit an old friend... Two weeks after I started again, I decided to go and spend a *weekend* in Angers

On Saturday, I left at the end of the day to spend the evening with Eric. We had an appointment at the train station. Curiously, I had the impression that he was avoiding my gaze. He introduced me to his younger brother Denis, a tall man. How similar they were! We went to dinner together. After our libations, the evening being well advanced, I slept at his parents' house. Eric seemed happy about my visit. He told me several times that he didn't believe it.

I returned to Chartres on Sunday. My parents disagreed with me: they didn't think Eric was the right man for me. My mother remembered running into him at the clinic and obviously didn't like him.

- Are you okay?" she asked me when I returned.

I nodded. Immediately, she whistled:

- I think you should not forget that you are grieving.

- Mom, I am not grieving for a husband. I am grieving for my children.

- What will people say?

- I don't give a damn about the others.

- You're not going to fall in love with this lunatic, are you?

- No one knows what I need but me, and no one will stop me from doing what I want. You are not in my shoes, and to imagine what I am going through is impossible!

I knew that my parents were very upset, worried about me and especially concerned about what people would say. Especially since my attitude was sometimes strange. I couldn't stay put. However, my desires were simple: to meet my family, friends, and in this case, to see Eric. He seemed to me to be the only one capable of filling this void in me.

The following Monday, I went back to the office. I had to keep my mind occupied for one more day. Every day I lived, every week that passed, took me further away from the drama. I asked myself, "All this time without them! How is this possible?"

Thierry, then Rico, announced to me that they were going to be again fathers. I didn't let it show, but the news touched me deeply. While I suffered hell, I accepted that life goes on in all its forms, among others in the form of a birth.

Christmas 1990 arrived. It was the first one without Lucie and Sylvain... One afternoon, I went to spend some time at Sylvie's house. She was getting ready to do the tree with her children. Julien, my five-year-old nephew, said to me:

- You're not going to make a Christmas tree, Auntie: you don't have any more children!

In his own way, in a roundabout way, he made me understand that he had noticed the absence of Lucie and Sylvain. He knew...

My niece Vincente, age 4, was at my parents' house for a few days. We spent some time together. She was drawing and talking to me about the imminent arrival of Santa Claus:

- Maybe Lucie and Sylvain will come back at the same time as Santa Claus?

At that moment, I was disturbed by Vincente's childish words. I woke up from my magical thinking. Until then, I was not in the real world; I had believed that "if I was good", I would see them again... And then I understood. The reality was cruel: no, Lucie and Sylvain will never come back. No, I won't be able to kiss them again.

Vincente also told me in her own way that she had noticed their absence. Children are easier to talk to: they are not afraid or calculating. They are more spontaneous, less analytical than adults.

*

I spent Christmas with my parents, at Thierry, Claire and their three children, Simon, Vincente and Aubrée. I was physically present, but I did not keep any memory of the evening. I remembered the Christmas 1989 when we were all together. A photo immortalized this festive moment: Lucie was wearing a red and black outfit that I had knitted for her, Sylvain was dressed in a mismatched suit. My father loved to sing, and Sylvain had the same taste for taking notes. That Christmas, with a hat on his head, he had performed a few songs from his school repertoire. I smiled at the memory. I was moved.

17. The surprise

After this Christmas party, I gladly left for Montpellier to stay with my cousin Jacqueline. I needed a change of scenery, to leave this heavy atmosphere where everything brought me back to the physical absence of my children and to the inhuman pain that I felt. Jacqueline and her husband are wonderful people of generosity. I will never forget this kind escapade. My cousin surprised me by making a reservation at a seaside restaurant for New Year's Eve. It was a nice day... I was lucky to have been so well taken care of.

On my return, I went to meet Eric in Angers. We were happy to see each other again, even if he didn't know how to express it. He gave me a statue: it was a brown woman, slightly naked. On my side, I bought him some sports clothes.

My friend had observed my environment, understood my determination, admired my will and courage. He alone knew that I would get out of this hell. Without him and, paradoxically, without his fragility, I would not have had the courage and the strength to undertake... Thanks to my meeting with him, I regained a taste for life.

When I returned to Chartres, I found my colleagues and my work. My days revolved around my professional activity. I took my bearings smoothly. Confidence was established. Today, I am convinced that working was an essential factor in my recovery.

*

I made an appointment with a psychiatrist that my doctor had recommended. At first, the sessions were short. I talked, I retraced my life... I quickly understood that he did not have the answers to my questions. The only person who could help me was me.

When I mentioned my next visit to the specialist, my father said:

- Shrinks are for fools!

However, I was not crazy. A great throbbing pain was oppressing me, undermining me, destroying me slowly, and I couldn't stay like that.

During my first session, the specialist asked me what brought me here. I hesitated: the words that came to my mind would still scratch my heart, my soul. But I had to. I needed to talk about it. So I said:

- My two children are dead... Their father killed them.

No response. I felt a detachment in the practitioner that was close to a lack of empathy. Our appointments were punctuated by "Tell me about yourself", interspersed with yawns. I talked a lot, my monologues went in all directions, but at the end of the session, I often felt lighter. The weekly visits became less frequent and eventually I stopped going to that doctor.

At the beginning of January, I applied for an apartment, and my application was accepted.

From my first visit, I felt comfortable. There was a hall that served the kitchen on the left and a large dining room on the right. The walls were painted white with a mouse-gray carpet on the floor. The main room was bright and pleasant to live in. The bedroom was at the end of the hallway, next to the bathroom. I had bought pink furniture and a flowery sofa. They harmonized very well in this universe that I wanted to be joyful, soothing and bright. I moved in February 1991 in this apartment in the heart of downtown.

I hung a photo of Lucie and Sylvain on the wall, but it caused me real pain, constantly reminding me of the violence of the drama and the absence. I then decided to take it down. Thus, I protected myself and the people who visited me. I wanted to avoid questions from people who didn't know, like: "Oh, are these your children? Are they at their father's house?"

The separation from my parents was painful: they were very worried about what I could do and what could happen to me. I continued to have dinner with them in the evening, in order to reassure them, but I remained firm for the rest and insisted on spending the nights at home... even if it took a lot of courage to find myself alone with my memories, my absences and my fears.

18. The guilt of junk

On *weekends*, I often went to see Eric in Angers. He didn't have a driver's license and lived with his parents. His uncle Roland, having taken a liking to him, took care of finding him a job in a factory, then finding him an apartment. He was a generous man and full of humanity. He knew my life story and seemed moved. One day he gave me a text entitled *Prayer from Latin America*. I was not immediately moved by this reading, for my mind was cluttered. The leaflet remained in a chest of drawers for some time. A few years later, I found it again, and the words spoke to me.

I met Eric's parents. His mother had a hard time living. His father said nothing. He just let it happen. Their son was suffering from depression. He felt misunderstood, unloved, with a deep sense of insecurity in his surroundings. Eric was a tortured, introverted person with violent outbursts. I witnessed many disturbing scenes. One evening, for example, he threw a bowl of coffee against the wall in annoyance. I was afraid of his behavior. I didn't know if I would come back. I refused to give too much importance to this incident, even if it marked me.

At first, he refused to come to my house. As for me, on the contrary, escaping Chartres for a few hours, my memories and my sorrows, allowed me to take a step back.

Eric's mother did not understand my attitude and behaviors:

- How do you, Patricia, have so much energy when your children are dead?

- I don't give myself a choice. What would it matter if I got worse? I keep busy, I work, I do sports... because I have to.

- You are unbelievable! My father died. Since then, my mother and my brother, I have a hard time with them.

She would go into endless monologues. It seemed to me that she was giving me looks of disapproval at times. I didn't like the way she talked about the son I was dating. She criticized him, was always devaluing him, and constantly brought up his suicide attempt.

Twenty-five years ago, no one would have risked a relationship with me. For most men, I had no future. I often thought Eric was "crazy" enough to believe in me and love me. Today I know that it wasn't crazy: Eric wasn't crazy. But he did love me madly. I dreamed of him, desired him, with as much determination as my distress was great. I would write to him, and he would answer me with long, moving letters that spoke of his desire to see me again. I would tell him about my days and tell him of my upcoming plans to visit him. Eric lived in my daily thoughts.

And March 1991 arrived. On the 22nd, it was Lucie's birthday, the first without her: for me, she will always be 7 years old. At the memory of this moment of happiness, my eyes blurred with tears. I was revolted by so much injustice.

My body was alive, blood was flowing through my arteries, I was breathing, I was feeding. Yet I knew something had broken. I felt that my heart was only half alive.

I regularly accompanied my parents to the cemetery. I was content to accompany them, because to go to my children's grave was for me an indescribable suffering. To find myself in front of a cold marble to think and talk to Lucie and Sylvain did not suit me. I went there to please my parents, not because I needed to, and even less because I wanted to. Every day, I thought about my children. I talked to them about the love I had for them. I already had to deal with their absence. That was the emergency. From then on, the more time passed, the less I went to the cemetery.

My parents often reproached me:

- Last week, we went to the cemetery: the children's grave is dirty!

- It's possible... I don't go there, it's true!

- Plus, it's not flowered. We put pansies on it this week.

- Thank you.

One more reason to feel guilty! My parents' words reflected their upbringing: "do" out of duty.

May arrived with spring, sun, party and Sylvain's birthday. Same scenario as in March: I was devastated. I said to myself: "He won't grow up anymore, he won't be a clown, nor will he smile like a little rascal! He won't come and snuggle with me anymore, he who was so cuddly..."

I remembered May 22, 1990, with this photo that immortalized it: Sylvain was with his sister. He was laughing. My gaze was on his, then on Lucie's. I could hear Sylvain laughing and Lucie saying, "Hi, Mom. I could hear Sylvain laughing and Lucie saying, "Hi,

Mom! The memory of this moment soothed me. They were alive in my heart at that very moment.

At EDF, for Mother's Day, the works council organized a special event for mothers. I was invited to this party, but I refused to go. I was no longer a mother, and I punished myself. The idea of sharing a Mother's Day with others was so violent that I couldn't attend. I knew my friends were embarrassed to both invite me to the party and not to. It was awkward, of course, and I was given a choice. It was up to me.

After the snack, the colleagues, to show me that they had thought of me, gave me a present:

- We have this little gift for you. It's Mother's Day!

- Oh, a bedside lamp! How nice!

I was really touched by this delicate attention.

*

This month, Eric found himself without a job. He still hadn't come to visit me in Chartres. This made me angry, but I knew he was afraid. Afraid of not being up to the task. Afraid of moving away from Angers, the city where his family and friends lived. Fear of leaving his apartment where he had his bearings... I had to provoke him to finally act.

One Saturday in June, around 11 p.m., while I was at his house, I said to him:

- We are going to Chartres. Now!

- Anything... I don't have anything ready.

- Never mind that! Take what you wish to take with you; and let's go.

That's how we arrived in the middle of the night in Chartres. Another period of my life was beginning.

At first, everything was simple between us. Eric wanted to get out of his nostalgia and lethargy. He had stopped his antidepressant treatment. There were still a few adjustments to be made: as a non-smoker, I attached great importance to respecting the apartment. I insisted that my companion go smoke on the balcony. Another adjustment: work! I encouraged Eric to look for a job. A professional activity is essential, especially for a fragile person like him. He had a vocational training certificate in cooking and very quickly found a seasonal job in a restaurant in Chartres, opposite the cathedral.

One evening, the phone rang. It was Pascale, a friend from Normandy. She was distraught:

- Patricia, I'm not well. Not well at all... I'm depressed... I can't get over the drama... I wanted to tell you that I went out with Jacky... We had an affair during your separation! You should know that the children were not unhappy with him...

- What do you mean, the children were not unhappy? They were dead! He killed them! Do you hear that?

- Oh, Patricia, I'm on antidepressants and sleeping pills...

I didn't understand. She was complaining to me about the situation!

- So, take care of yourself, Pascale.

I hung up and sat down, stunned, speechless: I didn't mind that she had an affair with him. But what did she want to tell me? It was impossible to understand the meaning of her call and her words. Probably. Feigned guilt? Maybe. But what need did she have to tell me about Jacky's condition at the time of the tragedy?

What had he told her about the children and about me? What did she feel guilty about? Had Jacky confided his dark plans to her? This call left me a bitter taste...

19. The other meaning of life

Eric loved Canada: he often talked about it and wanted to spend a vacation there. Together, we decided to go there in September 1991.

The idea was to rent a *camper* and visit Quebec. I went to great lengths to organize this vacation. He had no money and was not the type to go to travel agencies to prepare anything!

So life went on. The summer was moving on. I understood that my parents and my family did not look favorably on the situation, but they did not prevent me from leading my life as I wished.

Jacqueline, my cousin from Montpellier, was celebrating her 40th birthday in August. She invited me and my parents. At my request, we went with my niece Vincente, because I needed to be surrounded by children. I spent a few days in a small haven of peace. However, during the birthday party, I felt out of place. It was the first time I felt so uncomfortable: I couldn't let go and enjoy the party. It was as if I was not allowed to have fun, to be happy, to be alive, I who had chosen to live with my burden. I was torn between laughing and crying, life and death. Not knowing where you belong is terrifying!

September 5 arrived. A year earlier, my children had died, and I was experiencing the unimaginable: being without them. All kinds of emotions were assailing me: disgust, rage, sadness, despair...

Since then, every September, a feeling of melancholy invades me. I can't control it and, even if I want to, I can't. Nevertheless, with each passing year, I have more control over my emotions. I know now that, with time, the pain is less. I miss their physical absence, but I feel them so alive in my heart...

A few days after this grim anniversary, we left for Canada. Eric was thrilled. He was flying for the first time. I was amazed to be literally "in the sky". He, a little less so! Despite my enthusiasm, I was apprehensive about the trip and being alone in a foreign land. Fortunately, we spent a beautiful and enriching time. The discovery of this grandiose country, of its people, so linked to France, touched me a lot.

We landed in Montreal, where we spent a few days. For three weeks, we travelled through the Gaspé Peninsula in a *motor home*: 3500 kilometers of forest crossings, stopping at the edge of lakes, passing through Chicoutimi, Gaspé, Tadoussac, Trois-Rivières, Percé and all these cities along the St. Lawrence. An unforgettable trip!

During our journey, the birth of Thierry's daughter was expected. I knew the expected date, from which I phoned my brother very often to have confirmation. With the time difference, I woke him up more than once, until September 18, 1991, when my niece Marielle was born. I was sincerely happy about this first birth after the death of my children.

*

Back in Chartres, I went back to work, delighted to see my colleagues. Eric, who had finished his temporary assignments, was looking for a job again and couldn't find one. He started to develop bad habits, to stagger his hours. He talked about getting his driver's license and I supported him in his idea, convinced that it was the door to a new life for him.

- After that, you know, I know people in Chartres. I can help you find a job, even for a few months.

- No, I'll do it on my own.

He was getting more and more annoyed, and I could stand it less and less. I didn't understand the reasons for his unhappiness, and I found it hard to accept his passivity, when I was so active. Living with him was not easy. Very quickly, our relationship went sour. In October, we separated. Eric left for Angers. A few weeks later, we got back in touch and started living together again. How happy we were to be together again!

Then came autumn. I don't like this season. The days are short, it's cold, nature is changing. I was sad. Eric was living with me, but with one more Christmas to go without Lucie and Sylvain, I was feeling very nostalgic. I visited my parents often. I needed their moral support, their reassuring presence.

Fortunately, at the end of 1991, the accounting department was very busy. Thus, my mind was too busy to brood.

Since returning from Canada, I had put on almost 10 kilos, but I didn't care. The boxes of chocolates would come and go in the office: one day a colleague would offer a box; the next week, another would come along. I don't think I ever ate as many chocolates as I did that year! Sweets are a great comfort. They soothe the aching soul, and mine felt less painful once it was soothed by these sweets. However, I had a permanent nausea which I attributed to the abuse of chocolates of a famous Belgian brand.

After the holidays, there was no improvement: I was sick to my stomach. Eventually, the thought came to me: what if I was pregnant? I couldn't be. Of course, I had told the psychiatrist that I would have more children. I had a strong desire to have children. In spite of everything, I had convinced myself that I would no longer be a mother. Jacky had stolen Lucie and Sylvain from me. But what if nature decided that it was so? I took a pregnancy test and the result left no room for doubt: I was going to have a third child. What an upheaval! It was both violent and wonderful. Violent, because I was torn between the life that was taking shape in me and the memory of my missing children. Wonderful, yes, because it was the most beautiful thing that could happen to me.

I rushed to tell the father-to-be the news. As I had imagined, he was surprised and scared at the same time. He was going to have to take responsibility and make a lifelong commitment.

On my side, the surprise was also there. As it was good, I felt no fear. For the sake of my baby's health and because of the euphoria of the moment, I decided to stop taking antidepressants. Excited, I went to visit my parents to share my joy with them. To my dismay, they were not very happy. They were worried. They looked at me without saying anything, keeping to themselves the many questions that were burning their lips.

Then I told my colleagues. On the surface, they were happy for me... although some felt I had wasted no time.

Never mind the slander! From that day on, I knew who I was standing up for. Life took on a different meaning. A glimmer of hope now shone in me. A door was opening and I could see the future.

20. The little ball

Eric had made some friends in Chartres. Young people who were a bit fragile, lost and passive, idle, with no plans in life. Their presence did not bring any help to my companion. These people spent a lot of time at home and, in the evening, when I came home, they were still there. It annoyed me.

At Christmas 1991, I missed Lucie and Sylvain cruelly, but I knew that the next year would be better. I could feel my body changing, my eating habits changing and a gentle fatigue setting in. I had no doubt that I was going to have a baby. It was wonderful! I loved him already.

My pregnancy was going well. I was tired, so I rested a lot. I was happy and full of doubts. Life with Eric was scary. He certainly wasn't the ideal partner for the situation. Would I be able to raise this baby and welcome him with all the love he needed? What if the pregnancy didn't come to term? However, the baby I was carrying weighed on the right side of the scale - on the side of hope, life, love. I lived this moment as a blessing.

I reassured Eric as best I could. I kept telling him:

- We have overcome many trials. Together we can be strong. I have the will. You too must have the means.

He heard but did not listen. He didn't know how to live and behave like an adult. I loved him in spite of everything. I believed in us. I wanted to fight to save our relationship and to save him.

However, I was consumed with the baby I was carrying. As the weeks went by, my thoughts seemed lighter. I was breathing easier. I learned that it would be a boy.

*

I continued to see my parents and family regularly. Eric didn't come with me very often, which saddened me. He didn't understand how important their presence was to me. He was still talking to me about getting his driver's license. I encouraged him:

- It would be really nice, considering that the family will grow. Plus, you'd be more independent!

I was still trying to believe it...

In May 1992, Eric found a job as a cook in Chartres, alas, seasonal. He excelled at his job, he was a very meticulous person who did not know how to manage his time. When he was working, he didn't sleep. When he was not working, he was in a state of total lethargy. He was constantly in excess. He behaved like a capricious, demanding kid who couldn't stand being told no.

He was a big kid and I didn't deny him anything, especially since I was starting to be afraid of his reactions, of what I was saying... Eric had already experienced outbursts of rage towards himself, but never towards me, at least not physically. He knew what I had been through and how much I had been abused. Despite this, he did not spare me. On the contrary, he manipulated me, as he was a playful man.

In July, Thomas, one of his friends, committed suicide. It was a catastrophe for Eric and for me as well. He shut himself up in a world from which I was excluded. He sank into a melancholy that I could do nothing about. I felt alone waiting for our baby. I was carrying this child that allowed me to fly away to a more concrete future; nevertheless, I was suffering. I knew that I had chosen Eric and that I had to accept that choice. Our relationship was not the one I had dreamed of. I wanted us to be happy together. But did he want that? He didn't come home at break time. I would pick him up at the end of his work day, because he still didn't have his license. Sometimes, when we got home, it was midnight. I was tired, and he was absent, far away. He didn't talk to me anymore, too absorbed in the memory of his dead friend.

That same summer, I suspected Eric was having an affair with a waitress who worked in the same restaurant as him. If he didn't come home in the afternoons, maybe it was to spend time with her. The thought of this betrayal was devastating. I lived the end of my pregnancy alone and sad, even though I felt supported by the strength of the life I carried within me. I was clinging to this baby who was my rebirth as a mother. If Eric didn't want to be a father, I would raise him alone. That didn't scare me.

*

The birth was planned for the beginning of September 1992. On August 14, around 3 p.m., Eric wanted to go to Carrefour: he loved to hang out in the big stores, unlike me. He didn't have any money, but he liked to rummage around, to find good deals. I was not in shape, but I agreed to take him. And suddenly, I let go:

- I want to go home.

- Why? We just got here.

- I start to have contractions, and they intensify. I need to lie down.

- I don't understand: the birth is planned for the beginning of September, and you already start to...

- I insist, Eric! Besides, it's very hot!

- All right, all right, let's go home...

Around 5:30 p.m., there was no doubt: it was time to go to the maternity ward. The contractions were getting closer and closer and more intense. I gathered my toiletries, clothes for the baby and for myself. But my 25 year old son didn't want to come with me anymore. After many minutes, he finally deigned to come with me. My family was on vacation, and since my partner didn't have a license, I had to drive to the hospital. It was 6:30 pm. I was driving slowly, and I never found the time so long. When I arrived at the maternity ward, I was quickly moved to the labor room.

- It was about time!" the midwife whispered to me.

The rest went pretty fast. Thibault was born around 8pm. He was a beautiful little boy. I counted his little fingers, I looked at his pretty face. I was reassured. Happy to hold him close to me. Mommy again. I loved his little face. I couldn't take my eyes off of him, I devoured him with my gaze. I was filled.

It didn't take long for Eric to run away. After that, he didn't come back to the maternity ward very often. I was worried about his friends: his supposed mistress, his unhealthy friends... I needed him to be there! I wanted him to be Thibault's father. I wanted us to live well together.

My parents came back from vacation in a hurry. My mother visited me right away and spent a lot of time with me. I could count on her. Since I lived in Normandy, she hadn't known my two little angels very much, and I knew she wouldn't miss out on her relationship with Thibault.

21. Annoyance

Back home, I felt overwhelmed. Eric had never been very active in the household chores. He hadn't felt more involved since the birth of Thibault, who he said was protected behind his endless:

- I am not comfortable with babies.

He rarely took his son in his arms, rarely gave him a bottle... Fortunately, my role as a mother was important to me. A fortnight later, Thibault was still not recognized by his father! Eric didn't want to get involved before the birth. Now it was urgent, but he did not want to go with me. He hesitated, didn't know what attitude to adopt... I was distraught. I had to insist that we go with our son to Chartres. When we arrived in front of the city hall, I asked Eric :

- What do you want his name to be, Van Craeynest or Oddo? I'm giving you a chance to become a father. What do you want to do with your life ? What does Thibault mean to you ?

I was annoyed, tired, sad, disappointed.

No response.

- Are you coming in with me or not?

Eric was paralyzed by the fear of commitment, of taking responsibility as a father and of I don't know what else... Faced with his lack of reaction, I entered the town hall with Thibault, closely followed by his father. We were greeted by a city hall employee:

- We have come to recognize our baby," I announced.

- I need the family record book... What is his first name?

- Thibault," I replied.

- What about his last name?

I was hoping Eric would speak up. I stared at him. The lady at the registry office looked at us with a surprised look. She must have thought we were a strange family. In view of Eric's silence and the ridiculousness of the situation, I decided to make a decision:

- His name will be Van Craeynest.

At that time, my life revolved around Thibault, his bottle feedings, diaper changes, baths, and his rest periods. I lived for him. I found myself singing the lullabies to him that I used to sing to Lucie and Sylvain.

Thibault had a pretty white room, with a blue wallpaper. The colors were soft as a child can be soft. For a month, I could not put him to sleep in that room. He slept in his bassinet next to me in our room. I needed to hear him breathe. I didn't sleep well. Eric was annoyed because the nights were restless, even though I was the only one who got up to take care of *our* baby.

Thibault ended up sleeping in his room, but I would wake up to hear him. I was afraid. As soon as he screamed, as soon as he cried, I would go to his bedside. In his own way, Thibault reminded me that he needed me. He brought me back to the present. So I thank him for crying so often - so much for my exhaustion!

The days passed and, little by little, confidence in life took hold. Many must have wondered about my psychological capacity to raise Thibault. Bringing a child into the world is almost simple. Raising him, in this particular case, was not a foregone conclusion. Thank God, I did not have any doubts, and that is what made me strong.

I was living at my baby's pace. I felt good, in my place. I avoided thinking about my past, the drama. I had to heal my soul, and focus on the present by raising my child. In the afternoon, I slept with him. He was an anxious baby, probably because of the drama I had lived through and the fears I had passed on to him... and maybe also because of his daddy's genetic heritage.

*

Very quickly, I enrolled Thibault in the crèche. I wanted him to be raised with other children his age. A few weeks earlier, I had visited the place to make sure he would be fine. On the big day, I accompanied him to the nursery. When, after much procrastination, I finally left the nursery, I was not very reassured. I went home and stayed on the couch all day. I felt like I was abandoning my third wonder. I was crying. I was experiencing this separation as a heartbreak.

At 4pm sharp, I finally got my child back. Everything had gone well. I left with peace of mind... and I was able to go back to work. I was delighted to be back with my colleagues and a professional activity. In fact, I had no choice: financially speaking, it was necessary, as Eric did not have a stable job. In spite of his great availability, he still refused to keep Thibault from time to time:

with a child on his hands, how could he find a job? Moreover, he had to receive his many friends, as energetic as he was, who were always visiting him.

This notwithstanding, I felt good and that changed everything: Eric was better - or maybe I was paying less attention to his moods... So I allowed myself to leave him alone for a while with his son.

Thibault was growing up and waking up. He was a smiling, yet fearful child. He loved his environment. He was very attached to his habits and familiar smells.

- I'll always be there to protect you, I promised her softly.

Sometimes I would freeze-frame and look at my journey: conflicting feelings would arise, ranging from pride at having survived the hell, to shame at not having been able to save Lucie and Sylvain.

On *weekends,* I spent a lot of time with my mother.

- Eric, I'm going to Morancez. Will you come with me ?

- No, I'm tired, I'll stay here. I'm going to watch a movie.

He was afraid of judgments and questions like:

- Have you found a job?

Maybe he didn't feel he was up to what I expected of him - looking for a job to get out of a precarious situation. I never blamed him for anything, even if his attitude annoyed me a lot. However, I couldn't help but question him:

- Eric, have you sent out any cover letters? I read in the paper that they are looking for people in the restaurant business. Shouldn't we call? I wrote down the number.

He started taking code lessons. But he put terrifying pressure on himself. As a result, he took his driver's license exam five times, always failed, and therefore never got his license.

22. The Reunion

Like the previous year, Eric ended up finding a seasonal job in the restaurant industry: his contract started in May.

- I am happy for you. You're going to have a real social life again!

I was at peace. In the evenings, I would pick him up after work, but now with Thibault. Eric had a hard time reaching out to others. Men, anyway. But I knew he was a seducer. He knew about female psychology and understood very well that sometimes you just have to listen to a woman to get close to her.

I left in August for Quiberon with my parents, three years after I came there with Lucie and Sylvain. We were in the same *campsite*, with the same friends. I hesitated, because I was afraid of the violence of the memories. At the same time, I wanted to immerse myself in the last places that smelled of the unforgettable moments spent with my departed children. My memory was put to the test, because each corner of the street revived a precise moment lived with Lucie and Sylvain. Thibault was there, and that was my great strength, and one day I said:

- Grandma, for Thibault's birthday, we'll take care of the meal and buy a cake.

- One year already! How quickly the time has passed!

Thibault took his first steps in Quiberon. Not afraid of the water, he felt very comfortable in this universe.

We had a great vacation. My little Lucie and my little Sylvain were not far away but, that summer, nobody talked about them. What a sadness! I would have liked so much to be reminded of an anecdote of one or the other. It made me doubt. Had I lived this drama? Did Lucie and Sylvain exist? Was what happened in the last few years real?

I was in need of words and truth.

*

Back from Quiberon, I went back to work and household chores, without forgetting Eric and visits to my parents. My Titi found his friends from the nursery. The race had resumed, and I had no time to think, not even about myself, not even about the drama.

Eric's contract ended in September. I thought, "Surely he doesn't take his role as a family man to heart. I'll settle for that. I believe in us." Which kept me from asking myself disturbing questions....

Came the third Christmas without my two angels, and the second with my Tweety.

These end of year celebrations were weighing on me. I was torn between joy and sadness, between wanting to be with family and wanting to be somewhere else. I started to let a reassuring smile freeze on my face. I didn't feel like talking. Saying Lucie and Sylvain's name would have been an ordeal. I didn't want to disrupt the evening with painful memories and tears. A bitter taste invaded me: I had the impression to disturb by my only presence.

When the spring of 1994 arrived, Eric slipped me:

- It would be nice if Thibault had a little sister or brother !

Having a second child was not one of my priorities, given Eric's professional situation and his psychological inconsistency. I preferred to keep my mouth shut and smile at the idea of having another baby. I was divided. Then, in March 1994, I found out I was pregnant. Eric was hoping it would be a girl. Knowing Eric, my parents openly questioned whether this was a good idea. But no matter! It didn't take away from my joy at being a mother again.

*

As usual, time has passed.

Thibault demanded a lot of attention, which I liked. Now he was walking and liked to go to the park to see the ducks, which we gave hard bread to. He would laugh his head off when we went there. Mom's big belly didn't seem to bother him any more than that. My little boy loved to play with his hands and cars. He was always walking around with a plastic hammer and banging on pieces of wood to imitate his uncles that he had watched.

My pregnancy went more smoothly than the previous one. I felt less anxiety and went to my fifth month consultation without apprehension. I learned that I was expecting a girl! I was so happy that I had tears in my eyes. If Thibault was my rebirth, this little girl would be my confirmation of the right to be a mother. Life had taken another dimension. I remembered what I had said to the psychiatrist the day after the tragedy: "I will have other children!" This desire for motherhood evoked at such a crazy moment was coming true. I had the will, the courage, the desire. However, nothing was won, I knew it.

Life is almost always complicated. For example, my parents had fallen out with Rico, who had left his wife Nathalie and was living with a new partner, Pascale. They had a child, Valentin, whom my parents didn't even know. And, one day, in her kitchen, my mother said to me:

- Patou, Sunday is your father's birthday. Someone will miss him...

- Mom, it's up to you: you know the condition to see Rico again...

- Oh, that, never!

At that very moment, I decided to tell him what was on my mind:

- I think you are ridiculous. You miss your son and you talk about him all the time. You would rather suffer and not see Rico, even though he lives a few miles away. I won't be able to hold Lucie and Sylvain in my arms anymore and you voluntarily deprive yourself of your child. I really don't understand you. Wake up before it's too late!

She looked at me with big eyes. I grabbed my mother and led her to the phone.

- Don't move! I'll dial the number and you talk to your son. Ask him to come and eat on Sunday with his wife and children for Dad's birthday.

That's how they met again. I was proud and happy to have allowed this reunion.

23. Poor organization

In the summer of 1994, Eric worked for the season as a cook in the same restaurant as the previous year. My son and I flew to Sainte-Maxime on the French Riviera to join my parents, my brother Rico and his family.

It was Thibault's first time on a plane. He couldn't stand it anymore. We had a nice vacation at the *campsite*. It was very hot. Unfortunately, Thibault contracted chicken pox: he was covered with pimples from head to toe. So we had to end our stay earlier than planned. Especially since my sister Sylvie's son was born. I couldn't wait to see him!

Back in Chartres, I rushed to visit my sister to meet the latest addition to the family, a little Victor, as in *The Young and the Restless, of* which my sister is a *fan*. Suddenly, I realized that in a few months, my baby would be born. I couldn't wait for my turn to come!

Eric's contract had ended. Now unemployed again, my partner was not acting like a responsible adult. He hated one thing: paying the bills. But when he got his paycheck, he was quick to indulge himself and give gifts to the people he loved. It annoyed me, but I kept my mouth shut and kept the family going.

I had returned to work. However, despite all my willpower, I was tired. Very quickly, the doctor had to stop me. I had enrolled Thibault in a school that welcomed clean two-year-olds in the morning. I was going to be able to rest, because my Titi was a very restless little boy.

Mom had kindly offered to make me some sheets and decorations for my future granddaughter's room. Pretty flowers adorned the fabric I had bought. I was dreaming of a life in pink for my daughter... The birth was planned for December 24th. What a great "Christmas present"! On the morning of the 12th, I accompanied Thibault to the kindergarten. He was both happy and anxious. It was the school's Christmas party.

- That's nice," I said. Santa will come by this afternoon and bring you a present. Good luck! You're going to sing with all your friends.

When I got home, I felt contractions that accelerated very quickly. Eric was under contract for a few weeks and had already left for work. So I called my mom to take me to the maternity ward. As soon as she dropped me off, my mom went back to take care of Thibault, and Eric managed to free himself to attend the birth, around 2:00 pm. My little Angelique was born at 3pm. She was a beautiful baby, already very hairy. I was holding my child in my arms - total happiness. I dreamed so much to find a beautiful complicity, like the one I had lived with my little Lucie. Eric also seemed delighted to have a daughter:

- She has black hair, she is round and she already makes faces! he commented with a smile.

The happy father did not visit me many times in the maternity ward. Fortunately, my mother came often and, from time to time, with my son. Thibault seemed to be interested in his sister, in his own way.

When I came out of the maternity ward a few days before Christmas, I found the house a mess, as usual. I was annoyed. Suddenly, I heard a knock on the door. I went to open it.

- Hello, it's us!" cried my mother.

Thibault burst into the house: how I had missed him! We were very happy to meet again. We gave each other lots of hugs and kisses. When Angelique started to cry, her big brother realized she was there:

- We had to leave the baby in the hospital... I don't want him to stay at home!

- I thought you liked to kiss your sister?

- Yes, but in the hospital...

I realized that it was going to be a lot more complicated than I had imagined. Whenever Angelique asked for a little attention, a bottle, a bath or a change of clothes, he would say:

- Y'en a marre: this baby is always hungry!

Thibault didn't like me taking care of Angelique: he had a lot of trouble sharing his mom. So I showed him that he still meant the same to me and that I was only too happy to spend time with him:

- Do you want me to tell you a story, or play with Lego?

I was lucky: Angelique was an easy-going baby, calm, smiling and sleeping a lot. She rarely cried. As soon as I could, I would take a nap with my children. This way, I could recover from my pregnancy while enjoying these privileged moments.

For Christmas, we went to Morancez, on December 24th in the evening. The family had grown and, all together, we were now numerous. That year, we had decided to organize the party in the basement, decorated with multicolored garlands and arranged for the occasion as a reception room. My parents had set a beautiful table with a blue tablecloth decorated with gold stars. The napkins matched, and Mom had bought floral arrangements that made it look festive. A big tree glittered with a thousand lights and at its foot was a gift for everyone.

For once, Eric had accompanied me and even helped prepare the meat dish and the vegetables that accompanied it. When we finally sat down at the table, my father announced the program: oysters, foie gras and smoked salmon for those who don't eat oysters. All of Christmas!

The children played together and sang songs for the occasion, such as "Little Santa Claus". We took up the chorus with them, singing along.

I was surrounded by my son and daughter, and I looked forward to the future: "I have 20 years of responsibility ahead of me," I thought. I accepted these commitments with joy, because I felt a sense of fulfillment. Nothing bad could happen. I would always be there to protect my two loves.

I was going to sing for Thibault and Angelique, to walk with them, to read them beautiful stories. However, a shadow tarnished my happiness: the absence of Lucie and Sylvain. So I decided to put these painful thoughts in a box of my soul. I would question myself later. I had to live in the present and enjoy my new life.

*

After Christmas, Eric no longer wanted to be a cook. He wanted to have "normal" hours to "enjoy the children". It was a well-intentioned idea: maybe our lives would be better. Not convinced, I phoned Rico and told him about the idea. My brother agreed to call my partner, and after a brief interview he was hired in the family business. Alas, after only a few weeks, on his way home from work, my big, immature boy began to complain:

- It's complicated, I don't know the work. And then, with your brothers it's not easy: it's badly organized.

I had heard him talk like that before. At each different job, he had a relationship problem with one or the other, and he would find an excuse to clear his name. This time, he had opted for :

- You've seen the hours we work!

Listening to him, he was the only one who worked or "knew how to do". But he had overlooked one detail: by leaving the job he had mastered, he was losing his autonomy and his hand. The knowledge of his profession reassured him, he who doubted himself so much! A year after being hired, Eric resigned.

- I am not designed for the building trades," he admitted.

This unfortunate experience was predictable. I knew my Eric well, but I couldn't help but give him a chance.

24. THE HUMOR OF THE MARQUISE

My parents were pleased to buy a *mobile home* in Quiberon on the ocean shore. I like this place, I like the sea. The land was well located, ideal to stay with young children. I had so many memories engraved in my heart with Lucie and Sylvain, and then the first steps of Thibault...

The vacations were coming soon. I was very happy to join my parents with my two little ones. Thibault was going to be three years old, Angélique eight months old. The day after my arrival, my father went back to Chartres and the three of us stayed with my mother who was in charge of the housekeeping. She liked to iron the children's clothes and prepare good food for us. For me, it was an idyllic vacation. In the afternoon, after the nap, we went to the beach, Angélique in a stroller, and Thibault who gave his hand to his grandmother.

We were harnessed, between towels, snacks and various beach toys: bucket, shovel, rackets and plastic balls. We were settled on the beach. Suddenly Thibault shouted to me:

- Mom, look, Angelique is eating the rocks and seaweed!

Alerted, I rushed towards her. Indeed, she was putting everything she could find in her mouth, including the pebbles she had to find to her liking.

- Don't eat that, it's not good, honey!

My daughter loved the water. I had the idea to buy a small inflatable boat that I filled to sit her and let her wade with her games. While Angelique splashed around under her grandmother's eye, I played petanque with Thibault.

- Come on, I encouraged him, it's your turn to throw the ball, as close as possible to the little one in color.

He launched it... but far away.

- Keep your voice down: look where it's gone!

- Yes! It is far...

- Mom won!

- It's not fair!

Thibault began to sulk. Like many children, he did not like to lose.

Some evenings, we would go into town to taste a "niniche", a Quiberonian delicacy available in all flavors, even Coca-Cola - Thibault's favorite. The time of the walk back, along the beach, the lollipop was swallowed.

This family vacation made me happy. We enjoyed each other, the weather was nice, and when it rained, we ate pancakes with salted butter caramel or jam, and we played a game of horse. I was living moments of great intensity. There was no doubt that my path was clear: Thibault and Angelique were my reason for living, my oxygen, my balance, my happiness. I was living moments of simple pleasures, but so precious, after having experienced a drama. I was reborn.

At the time, we lived in Lucé, in a small house. We were neighbors with a woman, Martine, who lived with her daughter, her son and her mother. Her children were the same age as mine and I naturally sympathized with her... until this terrible conversation. Martine was telling me about her difficult situation. She was raising her children alone and their father did not see them. A friendship seemed to be developing between us. When I saw fit to confide in her my heavy suffering, she thought that Jacky had been right to commit suicide. According to her, it was braver than living. Her answer left me speechless. I was devastated, as if someone had just stabbed me in the heart. Tears came to my eyes.

Was it stupidity or malice? Or a (not very) subtle mix of the two? In any case, this reflection made me understand how quick, murderous and unintelligent some people can be. I still wonder: how can we talk about courage when a father kills his children? I promised myself to be wary of people from now on. I distanced myself from Martine and became more cautious. But that didn't stop me from having a temper. Especially when Eric did not take me seriously in the education of our children. I remember one day when I said:

- No, no, and no! We have already discussed the subject of weapons. I don't want to see Titi with a gun in her hands!

- Stop it, Patricia, it's a toy. He can't do any harm with it!

We argued, but the night gave me some advice and I put some water in my wine: "Patricia, you must not raise Thibault by passing on your fears. If playing with a plastic gun makes him happy, you have to accept it," I said.

More and more serene, I went back to work with good resolutions. I decided to pay attention to my waistline and to take part in sports. Five minutes from the office was the swimming pool. I started going once a week, then twice. I would swim 1000 meters, take a shower and go back to work. Between work and home, it was a race, and swimming was good for me, it was an outlet for me.

*

The summer of 1996 was the season of opportunity: Eric contacted the owner of the restaurant where he had previously worked, and he managed to get a contract for the summer season. He was happy to return to his world as a cook. As for me, a position of responsibility became available at the office, and I applied for it. The interview was scheduled for September. I decided to go with the children to the Vendée, to Saint-Jean-de-Monts. I was so happy to finally be alone with them... I explained to Eric :

- I'm going to take advantage of the vacations to prepare my interview.

- That's good. There, you are next to the sea. You will be quiet!

- Yes, during the day I will devote myself to the children and in the evening, when they are in bed, I will study.

And that's what I did for two weeks. The three of us had a wonderful time. Angelique was walking, now, and holding conversations with the neighbors in cheerful gibberish. She was all tanned, and her little face drew stares and recurring remarks:

- What is your daughter's name? How old is she?

- Angelique. She is 20 months old.

- A future marquise of the Angels!

It wasn't the first time, nor the last, that I would hear this highly humorous comment. I had learned my repartee:

- This one won't be blonde, anyway...

25. The charming gentleman

At first, Eric called me regularly. After a few days, he didn't call or answer my calls. I wondered.

The vacations ended and we returned home. I felt my companion distant, worried, absent. As he was often in this state, I didn't care much about it.

On the evening of September 4, 1996, we lay down side by side, and Eric said to me "without any further ado", as Jean de La Fontaine wrote in his school days:

- I don't think I love you anymore. Besides, I've met someone else.

I chuckled. The news hadn't reached me. As if I had not heard the words spoken. Curious, this mania for going deaf, as if my brain wanted to take its time... The next day, when I woke up, I only had a vague memory of the previous day's conversation:

- Did I dream or did I hear what you told me last night? Have you met someone else?

- Yes, that's right.

My body went numb. I was frozen. My mind was reeling. I didn't understand what he was saying. Suddenly, I found myself years earlier: I felt like I was reliving the same situation. For me, separating from my spouse meant losing my children, just like six years ago! I thought that if I left Thibault and Angelique with him, I would never see them again. The past mixed with the present. Overwhelmed by my emotions, I was unable to be objective. I was no longer thinking. I was afraid. It was unbearable. I screamed:

- Go away, I don't want to see you anymore!
- OK, I'm leaving but I'll be back to see the kids.
- No, don't ever come back, and stay away from them!
Eric packed a bag and left the house.
- If one day, you take the children away from me, I will kill you!
I was transformed into a warrior, a tigress ready to do anything to defend her family.

I found myself very lonely and completely down. In order not to sink into depression, I went to see the doctor, who put me on sick leave.

*

What I did in the days that followed, I couldn't say precisely. I would get up to drop Thibault off at school, and Angelique at the nursery. I would go to bed on the way back, I would sleep, I would cry, I was prostrate, unable to think of anything else but protecting the children. At the end of the afternoon, I went to pick them up, and the days went on like that.

I couldn't eat anymore, my body was rejecting all food. I had lost a lot of weight and energy. I was in great danger. Past and present were distressing me.

For two weeks I didn't tell anyone about the situation because I felt like a failure. I was ashamed and scared. Then one morning I woke up and said to myself, "I've been through the worst, I'm not going to let it get me down, I'm not going to give up now." With a determined step, I got up, went to pick up the children and went to my parents' house. I fell into my mother's arms, crying.

- Eric is gone," I moaned. He's met someone else. I am so sad!

- Listen Patou, you have to fight. You have the children!

I did not answer her. I thanked her with a look. For almost ten days, I had been walled up in such silence that I was suffocating. Thanks to my mother's support, I felt understood and relieved.

So I went back to work. Recovered slowly. Eating better. I was finally sleeping. I didn't see Eric right away. I called him often, but he didn't answer. I was worried that something had happened to him. At the end of September, I called him to remind him of our commitment to baptize the children in mid-October with Victor, Pascaline and Valentin, the cousins of Thibault and Angelique. With my brother and sister, we decided to organize the ceremony together. The idea of this baptism in common had germinated at its rhythm. The family was delighted. I was reconciling with my faith.

- Don't forget that you're committed to preparing the buffet for the christening! I told Eric.

- Don't worry, I will keep my promise.

- There is little time left to organize the meal, we must decide on the menu!

We had rented a room in the countryside, located near a pond. The place was very quiet. We had decorated the place with garlands and installed a sound system to mark the event. About a hundred people had been invited: family members of some, others, and some close friends. We had prepared many different appetizers for the aperitif, presented on a tree-shaped stand. It was beautiful! On the menu: monkfish Armorican style, roast beef with pepper sauce served with vegetables, a superb cheese platter and, to finish, a delicious cake.

Despite my fears about the future, I celebrated. That's right! This day had achieved its goal: for the whole family to have a good time.

It had been a couple of weeks since Eric and I had met again and I asked him about his relationship with his girlfriend:

- Her husband is violent and he threatens to hurt her. You understand, she needs my support.

- How? You want to play Zorro again? You want to save all the needy souls in the world! I need your support too. I don't understand you...

I was furious and, I admit, jealous. After the party, Eric left.

I thought about it. I began to doubt my femininity. His new girlfriend was ten years younger than me. I felt out of place! After this painful episode, thinking about a man disgusted me. I felt abandoned and betrayed. "I didn't want to love anymore", I told myself.

Fortunately, I adored Thibault and Angelique, and they returned the favor. I was going to succeed in raising them, even alone, as I had done, more or less, since their birth. Once again, I was challenging myself. I needed it to keep going.

*

On December 21, 1996, it was the birthday of Thierry, my brother. He was celebrating his 34th birthday during the family business Christmas dinner. It was at my parents' house, in the basement.

I went out of my way to attend the party. I met the sales people, the employees of the company and some of my brothers' friends. One man was very thoughtful and attentive to me throughout the meal, and I had a great time. I was touched by his efforts to take an interest in me. Until that day, I thought I had become insignificant, transparent, and I had become visible again, thanks to this charming man.

Alas... In fact, he was in a relationship. He was only interested in me because he had drunk too much! This confirmed what I thought at the time: "Men are all the same.

That Christmas in 1996 left me with a bitter taste. Without Eric, I was lonely and sad.

26. Forgiveness

In February 1997, Eric came home. He had left my replacement, and he had nowhere else to go. I agreed on the condition that he would take charge and become more involved in our family life.

I had forgiven his lapse, without excusing it. I still hoped he would change. "I promised myself, "No matter what, if we split up, I'll never leave the kids with him. I didn't trust anyone anymore, especially not a father. I knew deep down that Eric wouldn't change, but I was once again locking myself into an uncomfortable situation... which I accepted. Separating from Eric would have meant leaving the kids with him, at least for some *weekends*.

One morning when I woke up, he gave me the terrifying news that a man had killed his children and tried to commit suicide.

This news chilled me. I wish I had suffered enough so that such tragedies would never happen again. But no, the demented violence still existed. Through this story, I relived my ordeal and I thought of that mother: she would have to go through the same terrifying ordeal that I had gone through - she has since told her story in a book called *Touching Bits.* My fragile equilibrium had just been shocked, rekindling old wounds.

There were other problems. At that time, Thibault was in kindergarten. His teacher couldn't stand him and made him feel it. To the point that he would scream in the morning when I dropped him off. It was not uncommon that, in the evening, when I went to pick him up, he did his business on him for fear of disturbing the teacher.

At the beginning of the school year, I asked for an appointment with the teacher who took me in stride.

- Your son is a slacker, he makes no effort to reproduce what is asked of him. He does not listen to instructions.

- But, ma'am," I protested, "you're talking about a four-year-old boy!

I felt she was agitated. At least, she was talking fast and seemed annoyed. I was stunned: how could anyone say such harsh words about such a young child? I went to see the director of the school:

- Madam, is it possible for Thibault to change classes?

- Wait until next year: he will be with a different teacher, and it will be fine.

I walked out of his office, not at all convinced, and the situation did not get any better. Thibault was getting sicker every day. Finally, the Christmas vacations arrived. I was looking forward to it. One day, I met my sister-in-law Claire, to whom I shared my torments. She reassured me:

- My children are enrolled in a private school. I'll leave you the number and you call for me.

*

In early January, I called the director of the Catholic school. She promised to enroll him the next day.

On the first day, I was concerned. Would Thibault adapt to this change of environment? From the first evening, I was reassured, relieved. My son was smiling as he left the classroom: it had been a long time since this had happened. Thank you, Claire!

But soon after, I saw a fire truck parked in front of the nursery. It was total panic! I ran into the hall and met the nursery nurse who accompanied me to where Angelique was playing. I could feel her overwhelmed and sad. Thank God my daughter was okay! I took her in my arms and covered her with kisses. But why the truck?

- Little Victoire died of sudden infant death syndrome, a nursery nurse told me.

I was surprised and terrified. She was the same age as my daughter: almost eighteen months. I thought that the risk was only for children under one year old. I was wrong.

This sad news filled me with fear: "What if Angelique succumbed to this disease?" At night, I would get up and watch her sleep. Fortunately, time passed; days and weeks went by. The fear dissipated little by little and I regained confidence. For many years, when Thibault or Angelique were sick, I would overreact. A little fever or a boo-boo would make me lose my mind. I would panic very quickly. No one could calm me down. I had only one thing in mind: to find my children, because I thought I was the only one who could protect them.

Especially since my relationship with Eric was not getting any better. I asked him about his life project, his intentions. He said nothing. His gaze was evasive. He kept his head down. I was sad, because I imagined his moods. Yet, I still wanted to believe.

Then, in the summer of 1997, we went to the Vendée for a few days. It was our first family vacation, the first and only time the four of us went away. Every day we went to the beach. Eric didn't go with us very often. He stayed cooped up in the apartment and the vacations were very quiet. I had made children my main concern. My life consisted of satisfying their needs, sharing good times with them, and protecting them.

In September 1997, it was Angelique's first school year. I enrolled her in the same school as Thibault. That morning, I accompanied them, nostalgic. My son having quickly found his friends, I went to Angélique's teacher and I entrusted her with my little girl. I was moved, my little girl was no longer a baby. Now she was going to school. I saw her quickly integrate into a group of girls, and I was able to leave with almost peace of mind.

*

On Wednesday afternoons, I often went to Mom's house. When I arrived, I would say:

- I made a cake: we'll go for a walk and then we'll taste it!

And here we are at the edge of the Eure, in company of our friends the ducks. If it rained, we watched a movie. I had enrolled Thibault in a basketball club and Angelique in a contemporary dance class. My mother regularly accompanied me on Wednesdays for their respective activities. This allowed us to spend time together.

- Let's have a drink, it will warm us up. How about it, Mom?

- Oh yes. You know, it's not often I walk into a bar!

On Sunday afternoons, we went to Chartres to support the men's basketball team.

My parents' room was easily accessible, and Mom had a picture of Lucie and Sylvain hanging there. Thibault and Angelique often played in this room. One day, my son asked me who these children were:

- I don't know them, who is it?

I could feel my heartbeat quicken. Would I have the courage to tell the truth? I took a deep breath before answering:

- This is Lucie and Sylvain, Mom's first children. They died with their father.

He had a little car in his hand. He threw it and it came crashing down on the wall.

- Did they have a car accident?

- Yes, that's right...

I had been carrying a terrible secret that weighed me down. At that very moment, I felt lighter. But a shadow had just entered the lives of Thibault and Angelique. A brother and sister they never knew existed had invaded their world.

Soon, the children were seen by a child psychiatrist, as I wanted them to express themselves about the news they had just heard. Since Thibault knew the truth, he had become angrier and more temperamental. He spoke to me about Lucy and Sylvain with malice. I didn't expect this. I hadn't considered it. The specialist reassured me:

- Ma'am, you know how difficult it is to grieve. It's even harder when it's about someone you never knew, but who is so intimately connected to your history.

Thibault thought he was the oldest in the family and became the third sibling. Angelique was younger. Her reactions were less violent at first, but she talked about it a lot. As soon as she learned about Lucie and Sylvain, not a year went by without me being called in by the teachers, who were intrigued by what Angélique was saying.

*

From time to time I would run into members of Jacky's family. The conversation revolved around me, my children, work. At the end of 1997, I met one of my former sisters-in-law. Chantal was always happy to talk with me. I asked her about the health of my ex-in-laws.

- Grandpa is not doing well," she whispered to me. He's had surgery, and he's not in the best of shape.

For a few months, I had been wanting to call and visit them. When I heard about my grandfather's poor health, I rushed into action. I needed to know if they would agree to see me again, to talk to me. This was becoming vital, essential for me. I called, stressed as I dialed the number. What if they refused to meet me?

- Hi, this is Patricia. I'd like to visit you, if you'd like too.

- Yes, yes, why not..., my ex-mother-in-law answered me.

I was surprised and reassured at the same time:

- I would like to come with my two children, Thibault and Angelique. Is this a problem for you?

- No, come with them.

- Can I come by on Friday night?

- No problem.

I hung up the phone. I had to get ready to see them again!

Friday came quickly. Parked in front of their house, I explained to the children who the people we were going to visit were. I rang the bell. Mrs. Leroy opened the door, and we found ourselves face to face. Nothing had changed in the house: neither the furniture nor the tapestries. I thought this impromptu visit was appreciated, because my ex-mother-in-law was smiling at me. We entered the house, and I introduced the children.

- Can they go play in the yard?

- No problem. They will go to the chickens.

I accompanied them outside. I saw Thibault and Angelique running around, and that reassured me. I was very moved. My two children were playing in the same garden where Lucie and Sylvain had run. I joined my ex-in-laws in the kitchen and there we talked:

- It was nice of you to come. What are you doing now?

- I work in an accounting department that manages the nuclear power plants on the Loire River.

- How are your parents doing?

- Dad is always doing the markets or working with my brothers. Mom is doing well. She looks after the children from time to time.

Mrs. Leroy told me about her husband's fragile health, his last operation, his garden... We did not talk about our deaths. Lucie and Sylvain were not far away, I could feel it. Now I was relaxed, I was at ease and I did not regret having come. I was looking for forgiveness. Which one? Maybe the one for leaving Jacky. I didn't know. In any case, my ex-in-laws were not angry with me.

Today, I know that, thanks to this meeting, I have forgiven them: they suffered so much for being the parents of a murderer...

27. The enormous burden

In August 1998, it was Thibault's birthday. He was almost 6 years old and was starting first grade. Eric still hadn't found a job. I had in mind to buy or build a house. I told him about this project:

- I want to become a homeowner. I'm asking you one last time if you intend to move forward in life.

- I really don't know.

I started to visit houses: I didn't like any of the proposals made by the agencies, and Eric didn't participate. I decided to carry out the project alone but, financially, it was going to be complicated. One day, my brother told me:

- There is a piece of land for sale near my house. There is enough to make a nice little house.

The idea seduced me. This new project stimulated me. I was already imagining my future home: big windows, large living spaces, lots of storage... This house would smell like life. I was filled with hope. I was on the right track, that was for sure. But I knew I couldn't go on living like this: there was no way Eric was going to move into this new place. So I had to agree to let him have Thibault and Angelique sometimes, in other words, to trust him.

*

For Christmas and New Year's Eve 1999, I went to my parents' house with Thibault and Angelique, but without Eric. The months of cohabitation went by and became more and more burdensome: we each lived in our own room. I ended up fleeing the house, where I didn't receive anyone anymore, because the atmosphere had become so oppressive.

One day, Eric came back from the doctor with a disturbing diagnosis:

- Patricia, I saw the doctor. I am bipolar! That means that I go from a manic phase to a depressive phase...

He had finally found his illness, but the doctor was unable to prescribe medication that was effective enough to stabilize his patient's mood. Every two months, Eric returned with a different treatment. The house had become a pharmacy! This invasion was driving me crazy: Eric wanted to keep everything "just in case"... And I was thinking about our unfortunate children who were living in this psychodramatic atmosphere. It was hard for me to accept this situation: I was afraid that this nostalgia would overwhelm me. Besides, was this an example for the children? Their father was never available to them.

In the spring of 2000, I met someone. One day, we met at the pool with our respective children. Angelique noticed the complicity that we had, him and me. On the way back, she asked me:

- Who is this gentleman?

Clumsily, I tried to explain:

- A friend. You know, Mom and Dad aren't really together anymore, even though they still live in the same house. So, each one lives his own life...

*

Back at home, the evening passed quietly. The children went to bed. I went upstairs while Eric was in the living room. Suddenly, I heard Angelique calling me, screaming. She was no longer in her room and I went downstairs to join her.

She was facing her father... who had scarred his arm with a glass! I was terrified, sad and angry. Discouraged too. This would never end! When I came to my senses, I decided:

- It's superficial. Go disinfect yourself, Eric.

I ordered Angelique back upstairs and settled her in my bed.

By her side that night, I couldn't sleep. Angelique had told her father about what she had seen at the pool, and she had felt responsible for her actions. I held her close, hugging her tightly. I was disappointed in myself and decided to talk to Eric. This could not go on. I felt we were in danger. I knew he wouldn't attack us physically, but his behavior was still traumatic for me and especially for the children.

The next day, Angelique seemed to have forgotten the events of the day before. Safe from prying ears, I told Eric:

- Find an apartment and leave. I can't be watching your every move.

He seemed to understand but first wanted to return to the clinic where we had met nine years earlier. He stayed there for a few weeks in September and came back apparently calmed down. I reminded him that he had to leave, and he fell back into his melancholy.

At the end of 2000, a few days after Christmas, he suggested that he be admitted to a psychiatric hospital in Chartres, with the approval of his doctor. 48 hours later, he called me, begging:

- You have to get me out of here!

- What do you mean? It wasn't me who forced you to enter...

- It's a real prison, I don't want to stay there. You're going to meet the shrink. You will tell him that I was not well because it was the school vacations, that the children were excited, that I was tired, and that I could not stand the noise. You have to be convincing, I want to get out!

I sensed threats in his tone of voice and I understood that day that he was a great manipulator. I didn't believe what I had just heard: he was trying to make me feel guilty and to make me responsible for his internment. He asked me to lie to the psychiatrist and make him believe that everything was fine...

... and I obeyed him. I was disappointed, disgusted, sad, to accept to do things that were not like me. Eric left the next day. I was in a state.

- Eric, I never wanted you hospitalized. I wanted you to get better, period! What a nerve to blame the children for your unhappiness! I am so disgusted...

- How can you say that? I would give my life for you!

- I didn't ask so much of you. It would have been enough for me if you had wanted to live near me... Now I've had enough. Make your arrangements and leave.

Until now, for fear that he would try to commit suicide, I had obeyed his requests, which had the taste of emotional blackmail. Before he knew me, he wanted to kill himself. While we lived together, the same threat, latent, existed. Maybe he would act on it after we separated, but I couldn't feel forever responsible for his condition. When I realized this, I felt a huge burden lifted off my shoulders.

28. The unpacked boxes

In June 2001, the earthworks for the house began, with my brothers at the controls. On the day of the first shovelful, I went there to make this new project a reality. It was a great breath of fresh air... Until the day when the family business' storage area was totally devastated by a fire. The work had to stop when the walls were raised. One misfortune never arrives alone, my financial situation deteriorated. I had to start repaying the mortgage while paying for the children's schooling and rent.

So I decided to leave home at the end of the year, to move back in with my parents, while helping Eric with his housing and moving. He wasn't so bad and seemed happy with his new apartment. He was living on benefits. I felt like I was abandoning a child. But I had no choice... and I continued to take care of him!

My little tribe and I moved in with my parents, not knowing how long the situation would last. I relied on my mother. This calmed me down. When I came home from work in the evening, Mom had cooked dinner and ironed the laundry. I had more time to take care of Thibault and Angelique.

The children and I would visit Eric. At first, we would spend an hour or two together and have a snack. As the weeks went by, I decided to trust him and leave Thibault and Angelique with him for a few hours. When I returned, I found the children happy and fulfilled. Eric seemed to me to be finally invested in his role as a father. Thanks to our separation, he had gone from being a child to being a father.

*

In March 2002, the work on the house started again. I was ecstatic: I felt that my life was taking a different turn.

In May, I went to Tunisia, on an organized trip, with friends. Mom was going to take care of the kids for a week. I was thrilled about this adventure, as it had been a long time since I had taken some time for myself. The only downside was the feeling of abandoning the kids. It was the first time I was leaving without them, while I was going to "enjoy life". I called them every day, and when I came back, how happy I was to be able to hug them again! But I noticed that Mom was giving me the cold shoulder... One evening at the dinner table, as I was telling her about my visit to Tunis, she said to me rather curtly:

- You'd better take care of your kids!

This remark threw a spanner in the works. It was unfair to blame me. I had so little time for myself... Wasn't I allowed to enjoy myself?

One day Eric asked me:

- I would like the children to spend a night at my house. Do you agree?

I didn't know what to say. I wasn't thrilled, but I gave in.

That Saturday in May, at 6pm, I dropped Thibault and Angelique off at their father's house for the night. I went back to my parents' house, and I sat on the sofa watching TV. I waited for time to pass, looking forward to getting my children back the next morning. The past was invading my present again, making me very anxious.

My mother added her pinch of salt to my wound:

- I don't think it's a good idea to have left the kids, after what happened to us.

- There's no reason to, Mom. Everything is going to be fine.

I was trying to convince her, while I myself was not reassured! If I didn't want the children to see their father, they would think I was a stepmother. They wanted to see their father, that was for sure.

After a sleepless night, I called Eric and asked him about the evening.

- Everything went well," he replied. The kids went to bed a little late, so they are still sleeping.

- That's fine. I'll pick them up around 2pm, if that's okay with you.

- It works.

Eric was not used to taking care of Thibault and Angelique, and I knew that he was taking anti-anxiety drugs which made him tired and left the children to their own devices. That's why I was so happy to find them and to kiss them...

*

At home, the cohabitation was becoming more and more stormy. Three generations under the same roof was hell. I had a hard time finding my place, around :

- Kids, shut up, I'm listening to the news!

- But, Papy, we want to watch *Plus belle la vie*...

Fortunately, the work on the house was progressing, which reassured me and allowed me to accept this uncomfortable situation. My brother promised me to move in at the end of October.

When the big day finally came, Mom pulled me aside and said:

- You have time to settle in... There's no rush: I'm not putting you out!

- I know, Mom, but the sooner the better.

- You know, it's not always easy with your father.

- I realized that...

Very quickly, the children's rooms were arranged, and all the boxes were unpacked. I had reached my goal.

29. The new perspective

A new episode in my life was beginning and I could see a better future. This construction project had given a positive impulse to my life. I felt good in this cozy nest that I had prepared with care and love. The main room was bright and very spacious. I wanted to create an indoor garden. So I bought many green plants. It was a success!

I thought, "The kids are doing great; I'm finally settled in the new house. What more can I hope for? Nothing, really." The emergency was Thibault and Angelique: I had to be up to the task, indestructible, energetic, responsive. The busy days didn't leave me time to think, to question myself.

Every other Saturday, I dropped the kids off at Eric's house, which gave me a little time to myself. Some of my friends were lonely in life. So on Saturdays, we would get together for dinner and then go dancing. I had a wonderful time of friendship and sharing and I loved that time. I wanted to meet people, to change my mind, to have fun, to laugh. These evenings full of illusions helped me to escape a painful past and to escape the fundamental questions, which I was not ready to face.

Of course, I was always thinking about Lucie and Sylvain: I was sad, I was angry at myself for managing to find a little peace and happiness when they were no longer there. Then I thought of Thibault and Angelique, their little faces, their smiles, their childlike words, and I felt better.

But the bumps in the road did not spare me. One *weekend* when Eric was supposed to pick up the kids, he didn't answer our calls. I knocked on his door, a little worried.

- Eric, you're here, I know. Open up, your children are waiting for you.

Angelique was also worried, I was sure. She called him crying:

- Daddy, it's Princess, open up, I want to see you!

The silence that followed seemed like an eternity. Finally, there was the sound of a key in the lock, and the door opened. Eric, head down, looking sheepish, appeared in the doorway.

- Daddy, finally!

She kissed him and left to watch TV with her brother while I talked with Eric - actually, while I yelled at him:

- This is the last time you behave like this, or you don't see them anymore. Imagine what a state the children are in! Don't forget that. Be responsible!

By now, Thibault and Angelique were smiling. I was sad and powerless to control Eric's excesses!

*

A few days later, I was reading, sitting in a chair, when Thibault called out to me:

- Mom, I think Jacky had an accident on purpose.

His sentence left me speechless. What did he know? The answer seemed obvious to me. If he was that assertive, then he knew the truth. I took a deep breath, and then went for it.

- Thibault, I think you've heard some things, so I'm going to tell you the truth. You're still a little short, but you're old enough to hear what I'm going to tell you: yes, Jacky did it on purpose. Now I'm going to tell you the whole truth. It wasn't an accident: Jacky killed Lucy and Sylvain with a gun, and then he killed himself.

My son's face froze, and he jumped back. At that moment, I realized how much damage this terrifying news had done. Thibault fled to his room and locked himself in. I joined him. He didn't speak. I wrapped my arms around him and held him close. We huddled together for a few minutes, then Angelique came home from a friend's house. I thought I'd tell her about it after dinner. I didn't want to. No sooner had I turned my back than her brother told her everything.

Angelique burst into tears. She was screaming and seemed terrified. At that very moment, I realized how different my children's temperaments and behaviors were when faced with the same news. How were Thibault and Angelique going to deal emotionally with such a horror? I was sad to see them so upset and, at the same time, I felt relieved: everything was said, they *knew*.

On the following Friday, the children were to spend the evening at their father's house, but what was to happen happened. Thibault refused to move, explaining:

- Mom, I don't want to go to Dad's anymore. I'm afraid he'll hurt me like Jacky did with Lucie and Sylvain!

- My darling, you know now all the great sufferings that Mom went through. Do you think I would let you go to Dad's house if I had the slightest doubt, if I thought he was capable of hurting you, if I didn't trust him?

- No, of course not!

- So I think the only person who can reassure you is Dad. We need to talk about this together.

Eric called me quickly. He was furious. He blamed me for telling the kids the truth.

- They are too young to hear what you have told them. It confuses them! Thibault doesn't want to come and see me anymore...

- He knew," I said. Thibault knew. He just needed confirmation. His behavior is normal: you are his father, and Jacky was Lucy and Sylvain's father. We can't make them believe that this drama didn't happen. Now, you are the only one who can reassure the children and the four of us must talk openly about it: you, Angelique, Thibault and me. It's up to you to find the right words to convince them that you will never hurt them. We'll be right there. Get ready!

Grumpy at my reaction, Eric nevertheless knew how to talk to our children with tact and gentleness. Everything went back to normal: life and his daily routine took over. The children still talked about the drama from time to time, but very quickly, the subject disappeared from the conversations.

*

In November 2004, my mother lost a lot of weight. She was sent to Paris for a thorough examination. The doctor called us in to tell us the seriousness of the situation: Mom had cancer.

- The tumor is not operable. The chances of recovery are low. From now on, I advise you to enjoy the moment together.

I knew one thing: you have to love your loved ones while they are alive so you don't have any regrets. After her first chemo, Mom went into remission.

- I want to go for a walk, I suggested. Will you come with us?

- Oh, I could use some of that. The weather is nice. But we go at my pace...

It was a Sunday in March, and we found ourselves on the banks of the Eure with the children. The vegetation was in full revival. Nature was taking back its rights. The first flowers had appeared. It smelled like life.

Sitting on a bench, we were both fine, when Mom asked me:

- What happened to make Jacky do what he did?

- Nothing, Mom, nothing that could justify his criminal act. No one deserves to go through such an ordeal, you know.

"The big question, the one that many people must have asked themselves of course: did I have to do something for Jacky to murder his own children? Had I "deserved" some kind of punishment that fate had inflicted on me? Did I seek it? To this question, here is my answer: the earth would be depopulated if, at each separation, the father killed his offspring... I was the ideal culprit, since I had remained alive. For many people, I must have committed great faults! But I don't believe in *karma* where two innocent children were punished instead of me.

No.

195

Nothing can ever explain, legitimize or justify that a man is capable of premeditating the death of his children. It only proves that he was mentally ill. Not that his wife was guilty. The only one at fault is him.

*

At work, each year, during an individual interview, we were asked to discuss our objectives, including deciding on our professional or geographical mobility. At the office, the news was not very encouraging regarding the activity and the future of the Chartres site. I was wondering. What should I do? Move away from the Beauce region and my family, or wait for other people to decide my fate?

My choice was to leave. I doubted my professional skills and my ability to adapt to other people, in a different job, in an unknown universe. I thought that my colleagues and my superiors were not concerned about me because of my past. And then my mother was sick... It was she who decided for me:

- If you have to leave Chartres for work, go. Don't stay for me.

Mom seemed to be doing better. So I decided to inform my management of my mobility. One morning, I noticed that an accounting position was vacant in Toulouse. This administrative site managed, among other things, the hydroelectric power plants in the southwest. I was delighted: the Mediterranean, the Pyrenees, the ocean and Spain were all very close, and the idea of moving to the Pink City appealed to me. So I applied - even though Thibault was not happy at the idea that we might move! -and the Toulouse site was interested in my profile. I was called in at the beginning of July 2005.

After a week, the news came: I was going to be transferred on September 1st. It was a real rush, especially since I was leaving for vacation in Corsica two days later! In my head, everything was going on: I had to find a place to live, a school for the children, organize the move... It was a joyful panic. I remained motivated and happy about this new start.

Mom was pleased to hear the news. Eric was less pleased:

- You want to keep me away from the children.

- But no! I had to leave for work. You will see the children during the school vacations.

He was trying to make me feel guilty. Even though I wasn't fooled by the character, his trick worked a little!

- Eric, this could be an opportunity for you to get closer to your brother and return to Angers.

He was sulking, but eventually came around and followed my suggestion.

Mom was doing better. Maybe because it suited me, I wanted to believe that maybe the cancer wasn't as bad as I thought.

I visited a pleasant, bright, well located apartment near Toulouse. I was close to my work and schools. I couldn't have wished for anything better. Angelique liked the idea of leaving Chartres, but Thibault was angry. I too had fears, but I had confidence in the future. I liked the challenge. This new perspective gave me hope for renewal.

30. The little battle

Shortly after, Sylvie organized a surprise party with my brothers, nephews and nieces. That evening, my father, having a blow to the nose, was aggressive towards me. I was saddened by his behavior. I didn't understand and I didn't dare ask him why. The next day, it was time to leave. After kissing my father and mother goodbye, I set off with the children. In the rearview mirror, I saw Mom waving at me.

At the stop sign, I turned left towards the cemetery and went to Lucie and Sylvain's grave. I would not have left Chartres without saying goodbye to my two little ones:

- I won't be able to come often, I told them out loud.

Then I went back to Toulouse, and I started to cry. I couldn't forget my father's attitude. On top of that, I was afraid of the unknown that awaited me. I felt overwhelmed. Would I be able to handle it? I stopped at a highway rest stop and called my mother:

- Hi, Mom, I'm halfway there. Tell me, why was Dad talking to me so badly last night?

- You know, he doesn't agree with your choice. Plus he thought you wouldn't go to the cemetery.

- I went there.

- I will tell him.

I was stunned. I got back on the road, and filed those clumsy words in a corner of my brain. I arrived in Toulouse. The children fell in love with our place, especially since...

- Mommy! Mommy! Mommy! There's a pool in the residence! We're staying here for life!

*

Thibault and Angelique started the classes without delay. Then, it was my turn to start again. I got to know my new colleagues. They welcomed me very well. My fears disappeared. I found myself in a young and dynamic department. I was delighted. Of course, the men in the department loved rugby:

- You are already a true Toulousan!

- Why?

- You wear the colors of the Stade.

- That's right, I love red and black!

Very quickly, we took our bearings. Of course, I didn't have any friends there, but I was convinced that, through the children, I would meet people. I really liked the autumn in Toulouse, whereas I hated it in Chartres. The climate was mild and it seemed to me that I had made the right choice.

I was in a supermarket when Angelique pointed to a little girl and whispered to me:

- Mom, this is Mathilde, my girlfriend, I want to invite her for my birthday. Can you ask her mother?

I did it. Appointment was made for December 12 in Cugnaux. Angelique was happy, she who loved being surrounded by her friends. Thibault was not unhappy either: he enjoyed being the only boy in the middle of all these girls.

I met Mathilde's parents who became my friends. From then on, we always spent time together on *weekends*.

Life went on slowly, lulled by the mild climate. The children were very enthusiastic... except for school!

*

For Christmas 2005, we went back to Chartres for a week. The whole family gathered for this celebration, happy to be around a nice table set up for the occasion. A shadow hung over us: what if this was the last Christmas with Mom?

Indeed, a few weeks later, my mother relapsed. She underwent another chemo treatment. Unfortunately, this treatment did not produce the desired effect. In April the doctor told us:

- There is no more treatment possible. We can't give him any more chemo. It's a matter of days.

The verdict was in.

My mother was dying.

During the Easter vacations, I went back to Chartres. She took me aside:

- Patou, if I die, I don't want to be cremated: I want to be with the children.

- Very good, Mom. You did well to tell me what you wanted. I'll take care of it.

I felt reassured. That afternoon, she went back to the hospital, and I stayed in Chartres for a few weeks.

Mom left in peace.

The ceremony took place on May 18, and it was a very moving moment, as a family.

At the end of the week, I left for Toulouse. The children had to go back to school. I had to work. I was in a great state of tiredness, I was on the verge of exhaustion and I could not sleep anymore. "Patricia, you can't let this get you down now. The children need you," I said to myself.

I was suffering from the death of my mother. I felt so fragile, so alone, without her. One evening, when I came home from work, my son was in front of the computer and had not done his homework.

- Thibault, you leave the computer and get to work.

- Later on.

- No, now.

I had noticed that in the last few months Thibault had become more assertive, especially with me. He was standing up to me violently, and I realized that I was afraid of his behavior. "You can't let this happen if you don't want to lose your son," I thought.

- Anyway, I'm taking the computer, I need it.

My son stood up, furious. I was determined to go through with it. I found myself facing him, eye to eye. We were so close that our bodies could touch. The seconds passed slowly. It seemed like an eternity. My son finally looked down and went to his room. I knew I had won a small battle. I had to stay vigilant so I wouldn't get overwhelmed again. Proof that I did the right thing: after this event, our relationship calmed down. What more could you want when you're a mom?

Part Three: Towards Freedom

31. THE JOY OF BEING LOVED

I met Bertrand in September 2006. I liked his pleasant appearance right away. His character too, except for one detail, which was not a detail: this man was an alcoholic and violent.

We dated for a few months, but very soon I wanted to end our relationship. He couldn't stand it and told me on the phone:

- I will kill you!

- Me, you're going to kill me? I repeated, dumbfounded.

I heard noise and shouting around me. My children were in the room and had overheard the conversation. They were panicked! For our own good and safety, I hung up the phone and tried to put on a brave face. I promised myself that I would never speak to this individual again. Except that Bertrand certainly wasn't going to hear it that way. After his attempt to intimidate me on the phone, I was afraid he would make good on his threats. The idea of letting the children live in this climate of insecurity was unbearable. How was I going to reassure them - and protect them?

In the days that followed, Bertrand embarked on the campaign of harassment and threats that I had anticipated. It was so low and cowardly that I don't even want to recount the highlights in this book. Despite my attachment to the beautiful city of Toulouse, I began to consider moving once again.

One morning I called my brother on his birthday. He seemed to be bubbling with plans. I said:

- One year older, but you still look great!

- Thanks, sis! Hey, it's nice that you called, I had a question to ask you.

- I'm listening.

- When will you decide to come and work with us?

- Are you serious?

- Everything serious.

- Why are you asking me this now?

- We will need a secretary.

- It's a good thing, I'm looking to leave Toulouse, but I'll need some time to get organized.

- Well, we're not a few months away now.

So, in November 2007, I brought my letter of resignation to my supervisor; and on February 14, 2008, I moved. The last two weeks seemed interminable. On the day of the move, I drove to the Eure-et-Loir. Every kilometer I drove took me away from Bertrand and my anxieties. I had no doubt that I was leaving for another adventure, and I was thrilled.

*

Back in the Beauce region, the three of us moved in with my father, in Morancez. The cohabitation quickly became very eventful; and the situation did not get any better when Thierry had

206

a car accident with his daughter Marielle. This one was seriously injured. However, a few months later, she resumed her courses and had a string of successes. After her baccalaureate and her driving license, she found a job in a design office in Paris.

In spite of my worries and sorrows, I met one man, then another. I lived two beautiful stories. Unfortunately, I did not feel at home with them. I didn't accept the love they had for me. So I turned away, feeling that I was going down the wrong path. I had the painful feeling that my life was treading water... until that day in September 2011 when, walking through the streets of Chartres, I stopped in front of the door of a hair salon. I entered and explained that I had been losing my hair for a few months.

Delphine quickly understood my silence, my doubts and my fears. After a diagnosis of my scalp, she advised me on a suitable treatment. Since September 2011, I entrusted her with my head, container and content; but it was my soul that she was treating. With the rhythm of the visits, trust was established between us. We shared our sorrows, our joys and our children. During one of our appointments, Delphine recommended a therapist. It was a lead.

Nevertheless, I was not at the end of my bad surprises - words are weak. While I was waiting for Angelique in the doctor's waiting room, my cell phone rang. Eric's name appeared on the screen. A little annoyed, I picked up.

- Hello, Eric! I can't answer, I'm in the doctor's waiting room...

- It's not Eric, it's Denis. Something serious has happened to Eric.

- How serious?

- He had a heart attack. We couldn't resuscitate him. He died.

I was shocked. Immediately, I thought of our children. I knocked on the office door and went in to tell my daughter that her daddy had died. Angelique collapsed and had a nervous breakdown. We left with a prescription for anti-anxiety medication. I was also very overwhelmed, and was thinking back to the circumstances of our meeting. On that September 5, 2014, as he did every year, Eric had sent me a little message, "Thinking of you on this life-altering day."

When I told him the news, Thibault, unlike his sister, was totally silent for many days. Each one of us is taking it as he can, as he feels. Whatever our reactions, the grief and shock of losing a loved one are no less severe.

The funeral took place on September 12, 24 years to the day after we met. Eric was 48 years old. I saw my children overwhelmed with grief, and I felt powerless. How could I ease their pain? I supported them as best I could. Unfortunately, I knew that no one would replace their father, just as nothing would erase my sorrow at not having saved Lucie and Sylvain.

I lived with this feeling of incompleteness, of failure. I had to give Thibault and Angelique a chance to build the best possible future. Listening to others, I had strayed from my own desires without trying to understand why. I went through extreme behaviors: I was both strong and fragile, solid and vulnerable. My children had become more independent, which disturbed me. I had lost my bearings.

I saw no future, I felt empty, alien to my surroundings. I was alone. I had an idea, but I wasn't ready yet. The fear was still too strong. I took my courage in both hands and decided to follow Delphine's advice. I was going to go to therapy and this time I would go all the way.

It had taken me twenty-five years to face the truth and come face to face with myself. I was afraid of the words I was going to say, of the ones I would have difficulty pronouncing. I was afraid of the memories. I was afraid of the pain that would inevitably come back. However, I wanted to achieve the goal I had set for myself: to live well and find peace. Tomorrow, I wanted to exist, to smile without being ashamed, to laugh without feeling guilty, to experience pleasure without embarrassment. I wanted to live with the desire to love and the joy of being loved.

32. The Pain of the Past

The shrink greeted me with encouragement. More than medication or zen advice, this is exactly what I needed. From that day on, I went to see Laurent every week. I told him my life story as if it were a news item I had read in the newspaper.

In the last few months I had become a zombie, a robot that fed, breathed, worked, out of habit. I was so far from my emotions. Worse, I was afraid of this strange feeling. And then, little by little, I entered my story, my real life. Mine, not the one in the newspapers. With Laurent's help, I deconstructed my childhood, and cut out my life with a billhook. I understood that nothing predisposed me to this tragedy, neither my childhood, nor my youth, nor my family. In order to survive, I had accepted to carry a cross, a responsibility that did not belong to me. I had put on an armor to protect myself from the pain. Thanks to my therapist, I understood that Jacky was and would remain the only guilty party.

Finally, I laid down my arms and untied my warrior's clothes. I looked the truth in the face, the lies, the manipulations, the moral violence of this man who did not know how beautiful life is when you know how to welcome it; and I once again gave way to my emotions. As the sessions went on, I understood that Jacky had manipulated me beyond his death: in reality, I was an innocent victim and not a guilty one.

Laurent told me about Boris Cyrulnik. I read *Un merveilleux malheur* and *Parler d'amour au bord du gouffre*. The titles alone spoke to me. What they contained resonated with me. I became familiar with the word "resilience" and I understood a little better the extraordinary character of my attitude in the face of tragedy. I became aware, thanks to these books, of the strength that has been passed on to me by my history, my family, my education, my children. By immersing myself in the stories of other people who have survived ordeals, I felt less singular.

To achieve this result, I put myself on *hold* for two years. I wrote, I questioned myself, and I dreamed often. Disconnected, I was. Thanks to the life force that animated me, to my courage and my will, I lived a beautiful adventure: going to meet myself! I reconnected to myself. Thanks to Laurent's help, I learned to recognize the mechanisms that fed and poisoned my life: reproach, devaluation, the feeling of never doing enough for others. I started to identify them and began to fight them by saying "no" without feeling guilty.

I will never be completely healed, but I have accepted the death of Lucie and Sylvain. I have accepted to mourn. What do you call a parent who loses flesh of their flesh, blood of their blood? No word in the dictionary is accurate enough to express the loss of a child. But I also knew that the horror did not stop at my little person.

On November 14, 2015, a day after the attack that paralyzed France, Paris and the French people, I was glued to the television set. Filmed scenes of violence were playing on a loop, and the media repeated terrifying news continuously.

I was sucked into the television set. These acts of barbarism were both upsetting and terrifying to me. I thought of the families who had lost a loved one. This event connected me to my suffering, to my wounds. I prayed for each of the parents who learned of the death of their child and who would have to survive it, an abnormal trial of life. These attacks were an electroshock for me: "I am going to write now. I want to understand my life story and why this tragedy happened." I identified with these parents, with these victims. I wanted to talk about my eternal love for Lucie and Sylvain, who died so unjustly.

For a long time, when people asked me, "How many children do you have?", I would answer:

- Two, Thibault and Angelique.

I didn't mention the two elders, for fear of creating discomfort, and of being forced to tell. Afterwards, I felt guilty. I had the feeling that I was denying them or that I was not taking responsibility. However, I loved all four of them ! It was essential that Thibault and Angelique learn my life story. They needed to know how hard it was to get up every morning, how abandoned, how helpless, how alone I felt. From one day to the next, I had to face the absence of Lucie and Sylvain, the silence of some, the stupidity of others. I resisted. I clenched my fists and my teeth; and I survived.

*

32. The pain of the past

Despite my desire to write, it took me a while to get started. When I got going, I began to realize how good it felt to write, and I spent evenings and *weekends* writing.

During this period, I met Romain, with whom I shared sports activities. He introduced me to one of his friends, Liliane. Immediately, I understood that this woman would be a decisive person in my life. We talked for hours on the phone. I had finished the initial writing of my book and asked her to read it, which she gladly accepted. In mid-July 2016, I spent two days with her. I was apprehensive about that day. So was Liliane, for fear that I would be plunged into a tortuous past.

We spent hours talking, dissecting parts of my story that were not clear to her and, ultimately, to me.

As I left Liliane this July 14, 2016, I felt a great peace and deep joy. I had been afraid of death for a few months. Why? Until now, I didn't know how to explain it. Thanks to my therapist and Liliane, I understood: there was still a place in the family vault. In 1990, it had been designed to accommodate an additional body: mine. I wanted to be with Lucie and Sylvain one day, that was certain. But the idea of being with Jacky terrified me. That's when a project came to me:

- Here you go, kids. I will organize a day for Lucie and Sylvain. They will be cremated. It will be a beautiful ceremony!

- Nonsense... Why do you want to do this?

Thibault and Angelique both looked at me with surprise. I felt a dawning fear, incomprehension. I explained:

- You must know that I don't want to die. If I were to leave tomorrow, I would be buried in the same grave as Lucie and Sylvain, but I don't want to be with Jacky. I want to be cremated.

- I won't be at the ceremony, Mom: it's not my story," Thibault replied.

- You do as you please. What you say is not quite right. However, I accept your decision.

- This is huge what you're doing here, Mom," Angelique told me. Huge and mostly weird, but I'll be there.

I felt bad, because I understood that Thibault and Angelique were disconcerted; but I promised myself to explain to them again the basis of my project; and, during September, I asked a friend, Noémie, who works in a funeral home.

She confirmed to me that this approach was perfectly feasible. We met to discuss it in person.

- Patricia," she said, "we can arrange what you want to do and take care of all the paperwork. Have you thought about a date?

- I suspect that such an event cannot be organized for next week, I admitted. Nevertheless, I don't want it to be a year from now either.

- So, why not March 22? I think I noticed that it's Lucie's birthday...

- Indeed, this is a great date. Let's go for March 22, 2017!

After a few updates on the day's proceedings, I left Noémie with a serene, happy and energetic spirit. I wanted this ceremony to be a tribute to Lucie and Sylvain, worthy of their innocence.

*

An idea sprang to mind. A few years earlier I had attended the funeral of one of my aunts. At the church, Dominique, my cousin, had played the guitar. It was a beautiful, unforgettable moment.

I immediately sent him an email to ask him to play. He soon replied that he would come to play and spend a few days in Chartres with his wife. I added: "I trust you to choose the pieces. I want the music to reflect the love I have for my four children, the desire to live that drives me, the hope that tomorrow will be even better."

At that moment, I knew I was in the right. I felt in harmony with myself. This day would be a success. That same day, I shyly said to my brothers and sister, with a hesitant voice:

- I would like to inform you of my intention to have Lucie and Sylvain cremated on March 22. I hope that you and your children will be present.

Without masking their astonishment, they promised me they would be there. I also invited the people I had worked with over the past 26 years and who had been important in my life. Many confirmed their presence.

I was happy. I was still writing my book and remembering the magical details of my story, the painful moments and the drama, of course... I was rebuilding my sleeping memory. I was still going to see Laurent, my psychotherapist, who continued to guide me on the path to wellness. Thanks to him, I was able to "repair" myself, if not to erase my past. I talked to him about my life, my steps, my insidious fears, my children. He gave me the tools to solve my difficulties, to heal my wounds and to improve my way of apprehending reality.

*

November 2016 arrived. I was looking for someone to help me refine my text, improve my writing and comprehension. While surfing the Internet, I found the person who would accompany me in my writing project. After having read my manuscript, Thierry answered me:

"I offer literary *coaching*. We will meet once a week and I will help you write your autobiography, correcting mistakes and giving you general advice to improve your writing. Together, we decide on changes, additions or deletions to a passage. I suggest without imposing."

This last sentence made the difference. Very quickly, I expressed to Thierry my desire to work with him. This adventure pleased me, answered my expectations. I was persuaded that this experience would be beneficial to me. Indeed, the writing of my book was a real therapy, different and complementary to the one followed with Laurent. I will never stop praising the merits of writing and psychotherapy. Thanks to both of them, I have been freed from my painful past.

33. Smiling faces

At the end of January 2017, I went to pick up the small reliquary as well as the urn. I wanted to personalize them with the drawings made by my little Lucie and my little Sylvain.

On February 14, I was with my daughter, looking through my suitcase of memories when she offered to help me. For three hours, we chose, cut, assembled and glued the images. Together we managed to line the casket with beautiful colors that made it look festive. I was happy to have spent this time with Angelique.

The rest of the time, my life was organized between my work, my appointments with my literary *coach* and those with my psychotherapist. One Sunday in March, I invited my nephew Romain with his wife and daughter Automne. Most of my nieces and nephews had become parents, and it was great. I heard a soft knock on the door:

- Who is it?

It was Autumn. I opened the door and hugged her, before tossing to Thibault and Angelique:

- I warn you, I want the same beauty in a granddaughter version!

- Well, you've got a little time on your hands!

All kidding aside, I realized that I was ready to pass the baton to Thibault and Angelique. Yes, I was ready to become a grandmother. The idea of my children becoming parents no longer seemed far-fetched. This was a big breakthrough for me: a few months earlier, I would have been unable to admit this possibility. This change in perspective was a demonstration that I accepted that life goes on through my children and their future offspring.

I was right to do so! One evening, I was preparing the meal in the kitchen, when Thibault reproached me:

- You've covered us up too much: we're not capable of fending for ourselves. I find it completely irresponsible to have given birth to us.

- Irresponsible?

- Well, yes, considering the circumstances, and the whole thing...

- In fact, are you telling me that I should have killed myself?

- Not exactly! You're overreacting...

Shortly after, Thibault, who had applied for housing, received a letter in which he was offered an apartment. We went to see it together. My son asked me what I thought about it. I played it straight:

- I find this accommodation well located. It is well designed and clean. It has a separate bedroom like you wanted. It's an interesting proposition, don't you think?

I felt a twinge of sadness, but I was happy: at almost 25 years old, it was time for Thibault to become independent. He was ready to leave home because he knew I was getting better. Even my son was benefiting, in turn, from the therapeutic work I had been doing for a year.

2017 was going to be the year of renewal, for all three of us, I was more than convinced. The move took place on March 10. I felt Thibault motivated, and that made me so happy…

*

March 22 was approaching. I was both happy and worried. For some time, doubt had been building up in me. I had decided on this event, but was it right? Two weeks before the ceremony, I had met a woman to whom I had spoken about this day. Without knowing me and not knowing the details of the story, she had asked me:

- Why dig up the hatchet? Isn't this revenge against your husband? Why separate them now?

At the time, I was flabbergasted and didn't know how to respond. But the following *weekend*, I took extreme care to clarify the answer to these three questions:

    1. I have never been to war and never will be;

    2. I have no revenge to satisfy;

    3. I want to talk about love for Lucie, Sylvain, Thibault and Angelique.

I was nourished by love, not by violence, hatred or resentment.

The urn I bought was red and black: I like the combination of these two colors. I had in mind to write on the urn the key words that animated my life, such as: "love", "hope", "life", "eternity", "peace" and the first name of each of my missing children, Lucie and Sylvain. I was delighted with the result. The decorated urn carried my values, which have become my strengths in the face of difficulty, suffering and despair.

On the day, I got up early. I was at peace. It was raining.

After my breakfast, I got busy with the housework: I had to keep myself busy because I knew that the time would go by more quickly. I was looking forward to the afternoon.

At nine o'clock, Sylvie and Frédéric, my brother-in-law, came to have a coffee. As I did not wish to attend the exhumation, they offered to replace me.

- So how did it go? I asked them.

- Very good. We found Sylvain's stuffed animals and Lucie's doll.

- Is it true?

I was very moved. The thought that these little people, so dear to me, who were buried with them, had been dug up disturbed me. For a moment, I regretted not having gone there; but I guessed how painful it would have been, and I wanted to protect myself.

Afterwards, I went to a florist. I wanted to buy flowers for the ceremony and I chose a bouquet of seventy roses, of different colors, to decorate the small coffin. I came back around noon and had a quick lunch. Finally, I went to get dressed in the red dress I had chosen to wear, and I went to the crematorium in Pierres, near Maintenon.

*

The clock was ticking. It was time for me to go decorate the funeral room. Friends were arriving, family members were arriving. I was feeling overwhelmed and the stress was beginning to overwhelm me. Suddenly, it hit me: I had to get into the room where the ceremony would take place. I pushed open the door with the big bouquet and the picture of Lucie and Sylvain. Pierre, the master of ceremonies, welcomed me. He was a friend, and I was delighted that he was there to orchestrate this event that was so important to me.

I gave him a presentation of the course of the interventions of each one. The room was lit with a soft light. The coffin was on the right. I placed the flowers on a table and the photo of my children high up, so that everyone could see their smiling faces. The red and black urn was placed a little further away, in front of the lectern.

Dominique set up his equipment. He needed to prepare himself psychologically for this particular moment. As for me, I had to tame the space, soak up the smell of this room and collect myself. I understood that I had to focus on myself, on the intention and the goal of the day. At first, I looked at the coffin from a distance. Then I approached it and put my hands on the wood. For a long time I remained like that, in communion with Lucie and Sylvain. I looked at the photo: they were smiling at me. I decided that my decision was the right one.

All of a sudden, I started shaking: my legs were not supporting me anymore and my head was spinning. I had never before experienced such discomfort. Those few minutes seemed like an eternity. Something was happening between the coffin and my hands caressing the wood. Was it a new energy or the love we had for each other?

I started to panic. I wanted to live up to the event. A few moments later, I pulled myself together. I heard Dominique playing his first chords. He was putting his heart into the music he was playing. Peace returned to my soul. The ceremony could begin.

34. The fragmented heart

To make the heavy atmosphere bearable, Dominique played as the guests entered the room. Contrary to what he had announced, my son Thibault came, and I was thrilled to see him standing at the back of the room, trying to mask his emotion with a stare. The beautiful song that Dominique had composed for the event softened the atmosphere.

At that moment, I understood the exceptional character of the day we were about to live. Every tune my cousin played touched our souls. It was gripping.

Then came the time for testimonies. To begin with, I evoked my dear departed, the nursery rhymes we used to sing in the car, our little habits, our love. Tri Yann. Graeme Allwright. Our complicities. The unspeakable. What nothing and nobody can make disappear.

I also addressed Thibault and Angelique, thanking them for returning me to my vocation as a mother, and swearing to them that they had in no way taken the place of their cadets.

Then my sister Sylvie spoke to me. She explained that she had really discovered me after the tragedy. She was amazed at my capacity for resilience, and admitted that she had been moved to discover, after reading a first draft of my book, that behind the ever-willing fighter stood a sensitive woman who denied neither her weaknesses nor her frailties. Moreover, I did not try to hold back my tears when she concluded her talk by saying simply :

- I love you very much, my sister.

Then, Thierry took the floor and said:

- Lucie, Sylvain, we are all here today, your family and those who came close enough to you to appreciate the richness of your personalities, your kindness and your innocence as children. In the past, we have tried to say goodbye to you. Alas, our insurmountable grief and indescribable pain prevented your mother and all of us here from letting you go serenely. After many years of healing, we are ready. Lucie and Sylvain, you are present and inscribed forever in our family history and in our hearts. We will never forget you. Your mother is ready to let you join grandma Olga and our elders, and we are here to surround her and support her in her reconstruction.

Then he turned to me.

- Patou, my Patou," he said, "I want to address you in particular on this day that is so important to you. You are more than my sister. You are my best friend and my confidant. You know me better than anyone. You know that in our family we are tough guys, *rugby players*, construction guys. Like everyone else, we go through trials and tribulations, but we don't show our emotions very much, out of modesty and tradition. I myself am not always at ease with feelings and words. However, today, I feel like taking it upon myself to tell you what I think.

He took a breath before continuing, turning to the urn:

- Children should never die. As a dad, I can only imagine the intolerable hardship and pain of the grief you have gone through. There are no words to describe the unacceptable. This event, contrary to the order of things, has changed forever the relationship we have with ourselves, with our families and, finally, with the world we live in. With unparalleled violence, it reminds us that life is fragile, limited; and, at the same time, it reveals that some of us are born with extraordinary strength, courage and capacity. Patricia, rest assured, you are one of those everyday heroes. At Simon's wedding on January 15, you said in front of everyone, "I have decided to be happy." This very small sentence, so simple for the vast majority of people, resonates extremely strongly with us. These few words are so powerful that they make me want to shout out how proud I am of you. We are all very proud of you.

My brother then looked up to scan the audience with his eyes.

- So, look, look around you, Patou, you who loved Patrick Bruel so much ! he ordered me. Look at Angelique and Thibault. Look at what you have accomplished. Look at what you have rebuilt. You bring us together today to celebrate the life that goes on and that is worth living in all circumstances. You show us that healing is possible. Today marks an important step for Lucie and Sylvain, for your life and for the life of our family. You have taken personal steps to recompose yourself and move forward. You have chosen to put down on paper your emotions and your feelings about the trials that life has put you through. We discover this talent for writing that seems to make you blossom and accentuate your smile a little more each day. You will very soon put the finishing touches on your book, and I wish you thousands of new pages of

34. The fragmented heart

happiness. Sylvie, Eric, Dad, and all your family and friends join me this afternoon to offer you a little bit of our shoulders and help you continue to carry the world. For one simple reason, the one that Sylvie pointed out: we love you very much.

With a tight heart, I kissed my brother, and sat back to listen to Angelique's words.

- Mom, you decided to start writing on that terrible day when those attacks happened... You thought of the parents who were losing their children, and then you said to yourself that you had put your two eldest children aside for many years. You felt guilty because you had us and you brought us up while hiding your history with Lucie and Sylvain. You gave us everything, everything, even probably too much... You educated us in your way. Even if I could sometimes reproach you, I don't hold anything against you, because to live what you lived is unimaginable. You overcame this ordeal with love and hope, and you gave us the love we needed. Not many people, not many moms could have done that. You have limitless strength. For that, I admire you enormously. So even though I don't show it to you as much as I would like or should, never question my love for you, never.

Angelique turned to the urn and blew:

- Lucie, Sylvain, my sister, my brother... I didn't know you, but it's just the same. You live with us. We have the same fighting mother. It's true that we didn't often talk about her past, because nobody knew how to talk about it. However, I asked her many questions: "What were you like with them? What were they like?" I could see that talking about you made her happy You can be proud of your mom, our mom, because she never gave up. Giving up is not in her vocabulary! Lucie and Sylvain, you are the two elders of our family. Today, I thank you because I discover another mom: Patricia, mother of Lucie, Sylvain, Thibault and Angelique, and not of Thibault and Angelique!

With a small smile on her lips, Angelique continued her testimony by staring me straight in the eyes.

- Mom," she said, "what you are doing today, it took me months to understand the meaning and the interest. I understood its importance when I saw your eyes light up, talking about this long awaited day, this day when we could say goodbye to our elders one last time. Today, I feel a bit sick to my stomach. It's as if we have been living with them for a year, and they have been with us until this day.

Looking at the red and black urn, she concluded:

- I promise you, Lucie and Sylvain, you can go in peace. Thibault and I will take care of Mom.

I was beyond emotion.

In my fragmented heart shone a certainty: together, by our presence, by our music, by our gestures, by our words, we freed my little Lucie and my little Sylvain.

35. Love is the Guide

March 22, 2017 was a bright day. Lucie and Sylvain were reinscribed in the family tree. What immense happiness when Angelique called Lucie her "sister", and Sylvain, her "brother"! It was the first time she named them that way.

My life was transformed. The ceremony, which lived up to my expectations, gave me a miraculous energy. At the memory of this event, tears are still beading on my eyelids. I was flying, transported, I felt filled with joy. Paradoxically, I was still shy about expressing and sharing with others this feeling of happiness that overwhelmed me. I felt alive. No one could imagine the transformation that had taken place in me. Today, I know that it is necessary to have been close to the darkness to be reborn to life.

And then I dreamed.

A lot.

I dreamed that Lucie called me on the phone and that I answered her.

- Lucie! I'm so happy to hear from you! Will we see each other soon?

- No, but don't worry, everything is fine.

I woke up, happy, with an immense joy in my heart. My daughter Lucie reassured me.

Behind the words, I understood the extraordinary side of this dream. Peace was coming to me.

Another night, I dreamed that my mother was near me. She approached me and kissed me. A feeling of total fulfillment...

A few nights later, I found myself in a large, bright room. I was busy in one part of the room. On the opposite side was Jacky. I didn't talk to him, I didn't look at him, and vice versa. No violence, no hatred, no anger. There was total forgiveness. It was the first time I had ever dreamed of him!

*

The dreams were beautiful; but the reality?

I had never wanted to go deeper into the circumstances of the tragedy, probably to protect myself from a painful news that would destroy me, once again. However, after a few days of reflection, with fear in my stomach, armed with courage, I took the road to Rouen to know the truth as depicted in the police report. The librarian to whom I asked for it answered me:

- I don't think the document you are requesting will be available immediately, the file is old. If you wish, I will make a request and you will be notified when it is available.

I needed to know. So I asked my two brothers:

- I need to know which of Lucie and Sylvain died before the other.

- Lucie died first, Jacky did not want to miss it, revealed Thierry to me.

I heard those few words and they stayed outside of me. I had to work during the day, I would think later.

During the *weekend* that followed, I remained alone, prostrate, without desire. Nothing was important anymore, I was lost. I kept telling myself that Sylvain had understood what was happening and what he was going to go through. An atrocious pain was pulling at me. The truth seemed insurmountable. *So* I woke up with a strength of such intensity... Out loud, I berated myself:

- You're not going to stop there. You wanted to know. Now you know. They are dead. Look at how far we've come. Look at Thibault. Look, Angelique. And this book you're writing, you have to finish it !

I spoke these words to hear them and to integrate them better. With an inexplicable energy, I stood up straight. My blood was flowing again in my veins, my breathing was more ample.

Today I know the events that preceded the tragedy: "A neighbor of Jacky saw him take out the garbage bags. Later, the baker heard the children when she came to drop off the baguette, as she did every morning. Lucie and Sylvain were killed on the morning of September 5, 1990 by a bullet in the head. Lucie died first in her room. Her brother was killed on the landing, upstairs. Then Jacky turned the gun on himself and killed himself.

I was taking in this precise news. I digested it. The weeks passed. Little by little, I felt like living elsewhere. Very quickly, I found the ideal place, in a small town near Chartres, in the countryside.

*

In early July 2017, I moved into a restored former farmhouse. This dwelling fit me like a glove: spacious, airy, pleasant. Without a doubt Angelique and I would enjoy it.

Life went on quietly. I found it beautiful and wonderful. I went out with friends, to the theater, to the movies, to the pool. I was settling into my new home. At the end of August, Angelique asked me shyly:

- Mom, would it be okay if my boyfriend came to live here?

I thought about it. I gave in. Dylan came. He stayed for eight months. In May 2018, Angelique and her boyfriend moved in together, two kilometers from my house. Finally, I was on my own: the last little one was leaving the nest, the destiny of any parent... I accepted this idea.

My book was always on *stand-by*. In the last few months, I didn't look at it anymore, I didn't read it again. Writing was a real accomplishment, a total outlet, it gave meaning to my life. The last few months had been energy consuming, and I was afraid I wouldn't be able to go any further in my process. The goal was reached for me, the children and my family. I wondered: why publish it, not only for my loved ones but also for the world? Why deliver my life story, intimate, full of depth, sincere, written with all my heart?

Days of reflection later, the answer was clear: my autobiography would be published. I got back in touch with Thierry, my *coach*, and, after a few hours of proofreading, modifications and final adjustments, the result seemed optimal.

*

In September 2018, the weather was nice, it was the flea market in Morancez. In the company of my father, I was wandering in the aisles of this flea market where many people knew Dad... when a friend approached me and introduced me to Cathy. I found myself facing a young woman of about forty years old, intimidated. For a few weeks, Cathy had been contacting me often *via* social networks. Her daughter had passed away a year earlier. We talked about our children. Cathy explained to me that she could never mourn her daughter. I thought that this meeting between two mothers bruised in their flesh, in the middle of a flea market, had something incongruous and strong. After a few exchanges, we separated and I suggested to my father to go for a drink. We sat down next to a young couple, and my father struck up a conversation with them, until he started singing "Vole, colombe", his favorite song performed by Tino Rossi.

If I were the dove with white wings,
I would fly straight to my love,
I would fly straight to the one who, from the Sainte-Chapelle,
pray that one day I will be near her again.
Fly, dove, to my beautiful one,
tell him that one day I will come back,
tell her the love I have for her
and I will never forget it!

I looked at my father with tears in my eyes. At that moment, I knew he was thinking about Mom.

Our tablemate congratulated him and then told us:

- I wish the weather was this nice next Saturday. We are getting married on September 15. By the way, let me introduce you to Jean-Marc, my companion. I'm Lucie.

- Oh, I love this name! My grandmother's name was Lucie; my middle name is Lucie; my oldest daughter was Lucie; and Angelique's middle name is also Lucie! I am writing my autobiography, which is about how I survived the death of my first two children.

My neighbor looked at me intensely and blurted out:

- I don't think it's a coincidence that you are sitting at this table. We decided to get married on September 15, because that's our daughter's birthday when she passed away. This was our way of winking at her.

- Great idea! Your daughter will be present at this wonderful moment, I know it.

A real emotion reigned around this table. As we parted, we embraced. I could not believe it! In the middle of this flea market, nothing suggested such an encounter. In only two hours, I crossed the path of two women in mourning of their child. Providence? coincidence? chance? What does it matter? From then on, I was aware of the strength that animated me.

*

Invited to a friend's house and in the effervescence of my life, rich with the transformations that had taken place in me since the writing of my manuscript, I felt like telling what I had been living for a few months.

Speaking was not my job. I often started a sentence without finishing it. I didn't know how to defend ideas, even those that

I thought were honorable and well-founded. This time, I spoke about the tragedy, I described my children, I recounted some of the events of my life, my struggle, the love of life, the trust, the hope for the best to come and the forgiveness. I was comfortable with the words I was saying.

The questions came up: How can you forgive such an act? Where did you get the strength to continue? Why did you write this book? And why did you publish it? The audience listened to me with rapt attention.

In December 2018, I met Marie-Christine, a sophrologist. After a few individual sessions, I joined a group. It was the beginning of a new adventure.

Dynamic sophrology imposed itself to me with force, from the first session. The regular practice allows to learn to live in harmony with oneself by becoming aware of oneself in its totality. Very quickly, the idea of training myself in this discipline was born. Thus, in September 2019, I started a training in a specialized school.

*

The writing of this book is my last delivery, the one of my deep pain. It is a deliverance, a moment of heartbreak, separation, suffering, and the prelude to a great happiness. I live this moment. Finally, I am free. This pain has vanished. Lucie and Sylvain joined the Paradise. Their place in my heart is right.

I have regained my self-esteem and love for myself. I am proud because once again I have completed my project. I know that I have to bring my story to a close, but I am certain that each day I will live will be a source of personal enrichment. I will keep listening to myself so that I don't lose myself again. This book has been an indispensable shock and today I thank God for having carried me all these years.

I took off all my chains, lifted all the taboos and untied all the tongues. I resurrected the past to face reality and finally taste the present.

And the present is Thibault and Angelique. My two loves, you carry this story within you, even if you are not fully aware of it.

Remember that love guides our path.

I love you.

Epilogue: My ways to overcome despair

The love

The unconditional and eternal love that I have for Lucie and Sylvain gave me the strength to continue. I wanted to live because, as long as I am alive, through me, my beloved children will live. How can I imagine that love is no longer there because the physical body no longer exists? The love, care and protection of my family also helped me to survive. I fed on love: a bulwark against extreme suffering.

Choose life

As soon as I knew that Lucie and Sylvain were dead, without thinking, spontaneously, I decided to continue living. How, I didn't know. But I would live! To commit suicide or to let myself die would have been an additional ordeal for my loved ones.

Respect for life

Even though I have gone through inhuman ordeals, I love and respect the life I received from my mother and father. The love of life, of nature and its wonders, of the human being with his qualities and his defects, has always given me the desire to go further.

Courage and perseverance

I found extraordinary resources to face the death of Lucie and Sylvain. When I made a choice, I assumed it and I followed through on my commitment with determination and tenacity. When I reached my goal, I felt satisfaction and pride. When I gave up - because yes, there were times when I was discouraged, bruised, hurt, overwhelmed - I said to myself: "Look at how far we've come! You're not going to stop now! Look at all you've accomplished!" Then I would lift my head up and move forward, looking ahead.

Faith

After the tragedy, anger began to overcome me. I asked myself, "Why does God allow little angels to die?" It was so unfair and incomprehensible. Doesn't the Catholic religion say that you have to atone for your sins? What did I do to go through such a hell?

However, I was right to leave Jacky. By killing Lucie and Sylvain, he was trying to punish me for leaving him, no doubt. Killing the children was his way of hurting and bruising me deeply.

Unexpectedly, I quickly felt animated by a strength, a faith and an energy that I have never lacked. Where did it come from?

Thibault was born, then Angelique. The birth of each of them reconciled me with the role of mother that I had been robbed of. My view of religion was then transformed. I am convinced that Lucie and Sylvain carried me, guided me. Or perhaps it was that the love we shared so strongly shone through to show me the way?

The hope

They say, "Hope is life". Throughout the years, I have always been driven by the hope that the day ahead would be better than the last. The hope of achieving my goal has helped me move towards the ultimate goal: to finally live in peace with myself.

Trust

After the tragedy, I immediately put my trust in others: I loved Eric. To trust is to give oneself a chance to find a little happiness. And I believed in my success. I didn't know where this certainty came from, but I knew that I would succeed in overcoming this chaos, which was the source of life. Just as after a war or a disaster, after a tragedy, life is always reborn.

Don't care what people say

As best I could, I left out what others were thinking and saying. Of course, there were times when I felt overwhelmed by some of the derogatory or insulting comments. Today, to the backbiters and villains who are surprised that I did not commit suicide, I will simply answer that it is unimaginable to put oneself in the place of the other. Impossible to understand and to live in my place what seemed to me to be unthinkable and unbearable before the drama: to live without Lucie and Sylvain.

Bringing luck

Strangely enough, I think I was very lucky. After such an ordeal, I could have sunk into depression and the pitfalls of medication, alcohol or drugs. It was the opposite that happened. I survived. On my own. And I remained myself.

The writing

Through words, I had to express the suffering that prevented me from living serenely. It became essential that this suffering became palpable, visible, readable, so that I could understand it and fight it. It also had to be known and recognized by those around me... and beyond. It took a lot of courage to deliver intimate, privileged and precious moments of my life. Writing has allowed me to reclaim sleeping memories. Thanks to this text, I better understand the admiration I saw in the eyes of so many of my interlocutors.

Forgiveness

Is it possible to forgive the unforgivable? In theory, yes, as Olivier Clerc has shown in *Peut-on tout pardonner?* (Eyrolles, 2015)... and in practice, yes: I have experienced it. Forgiveness is not a gift to the other; it is a gift we give to ourselves. For me, forgiveness is the way I found to cut the link with Jacky. In order to continue to move forward and survive, I relieved my heart of feelings like revenge and anger, to make room for love. Life must remain Love.

The sport

Sport has always been an integral part of my life. Sporting activities have allowed me to evacuate the pressure that very often put me out of my mind.

The benevolent meetings

I could no longer continue to live in this body that was no longer breathing, in which I was cramped. I had to meet Delphine in order to meet Laurent, my psychotherapist. I also had to meet Romain to get to know Liliane. Meetings do not happen by chance. I heard the benevolent silences; I grasped the extended hands. Thierry, my *coach*, confirmed my choice. Each one of them, with their personality, their skills, their tolerance, their humanity, helped me find the path to my rebirth.

Table of Contents

Epilogue: My ways to overcome despair

Part Three: Towards Freedom

Best sellers Max Milo Editions

Hitler's banker, Jean-François Bouchard

Confessions of a forger, Éric Piedoie Le Tiec

The Koran and the flesh, Ludovic-Mohamed Zahed

Governing by fake news, Jacques Baud

Governing by chaos, Collectif

A political history of food, Paul Ariès

Mad in U.S.A.: The ravages of the "American model",
Michel Desmurget

Mondial soccer club geopolitics, Kévin Veyssière

Putin: Game master?, Jacques Braud

Treatise on the three impostors: Moses, Jesus, Muhammad,
The Spirit of Spinoza

TV Lobotomy, Michel Desmurget